A.D.
a trilogy on the life of Jesus Christ

Edwin Morgan

A.D.

a trilogy on the life of Jesus Christ

Ἰδοὺ ὁ ἄνθρωπος

CARCANET

First published by
Carcanet Press Limited
4th Floor, Conavon Court
12-16 Blackfriars Street
Manchester M3 5BQ

A CIP catalogue record for this book
is available from the British Library.

ISBN 1 85754 464 1

The publisher acknowledges financial
assistance from the Arts Council of England.

Set in 10pt Times Roman by Bryan Williamson, Frome

Printed and bound in England by SRP Ltd, Exeter.

A.D.

The Early Years

The Cast
(*in order of appearance*)

The Three Magi (GASPAR, MELCHIOR, and BALTHAZAR)
JOSEPH, father of Jesus
JAMES, brother of Jesus
JESUS of Nazareth
MARY, mother of Jesus
RUTH, sister of Jesus
JO, brother of Jesus
SIMON, brother of Jesus
CENTURION I
JUDE, brother of Jesus
NAHUM, a Zealot
MARCIUS, a Roman overseer
MENEMHET, an Egyptian builder
SHAZ, a Babylonian builder
VALERIUS, a Roman house-owner
AGATHON, a Greek theatre director
HELEN, sister of Agathon
JOHN THE BAPTIZER
CENTURION II
SATAN

Soldiers, Citizens, Zealots, Actors, Prostitutes, Gamblers, Wrestlers, Processional Characters

The scene is set in Persia, Palestine, and Egypt

Prologue

Persia. A mountain observatory. View of starry sky.
Enter GASPAR, MELCHIOR, *and* BALTHAZAR, *astronomers.*
Wine is circulated.

GASPAR

    So welcome once again, my friends. No one
    Is tired yet of these annual reunions?

MELCHIOR

    Certainly not. I learn something each time.
    I love this cool retreat among the hills
    After India, all sweat and elephants!

BALTHAZAR

    I like the contrast too, after Arabia.
    Not that I'll hear a word against Arabia.
    Visions are born in the sands of Arabia.

MELCHIOR

    In India as well! Don't get me wrong!
    A wise man learns from every living thing.

GASPAR

    Meanwhile we are here, with our friends the stars,
    In Zoroaster's harsh, lush – which is it? – land,
    Land of light and darkness and the eternal
    Unwinnable spiritual war between them.
    I leave that war to others. My job is stars.
    You know I think they are really quite far off.

MELCHIOR

    How far? Tens of miles? Hundreds?

GASPAR

    What do you say to thousands, many thousands?

MELCHIOR
    Oh –

GASPAR
            Why not? Think of the numbers.
    They are not jostling, they need space.
    They are not cloves stuck in an orange.
    There is a universe out there, big enough
    Not to be shaken by wars of light and darkness.

BALTHAZAR
    You Persians are obsessed with light and darkness!

GASPAR
    And so we should be. There must be dialectic.
    If there was one law, that would be the end,
    One revelation, we could shut up shop.
    The world breathes in and out. *Odi et amo.*

BALTHAZAR
    Latin next! An education coming here.

GASPAR
    Catullus, a poet: you should read him.
    As I was saying, the universe is large,
    Varied, and not without change. Trusty,
    You constellations out there, are you?
    Up to a point, up to a point. We three,
    Observers, questioners, measurers,
    Must always look for the unplanned event
    In an alive-and-kicking universe.

BALTHAZAR
    And note it.

MELCHIOR
            And remember it. Like –

GASPAR
    Like our great triangulation trek,
    When we had climbed Mounts Ararat and Hermon
    And had come down south through Galilee
    To cut across to our last point, Mount Carmel.
    By the light, it must be fifteen years or more.
    Anyhow, it still seems fresh to me –

MELCHIOR
    And me –

BALTHAZAR
                No doubt about it –

GASPAR
                                  We had stopped
    At a small town called Nazareth –

MELCHIOR
                            Bethlehem –

GASPAR
    No no, it was Nazareth, I remember clearly.
    On a hill, no great place, but the countryside
    Fertile round about. And that great star
    We had stopped for –

BALTHAZAR
                      Never seen such brilliance –

MELCHIOR
    It flashed where there was nothing before
    (At least as far as we could see), exploded
    Very suddenly, but not so suddenly
    That we failed to note down its position –

GASPAR
    A nova, as our Chinese friends confirmed.
    I think we had just set down our instruments
    When we heard a baby cry, is that right?

BALTHAZAR
   That's right. It seemed so strange: new star, new baby.

GASPAR
   The cry came from a cave, didn't it?
   There they were, as we came closer, mother,
   Baby, small fire, oil-lamp, silence
   Apart from the rumour of the nearby town.
   Wasn't it like a picture, framed
   By the rock, with the flickering flames
   Throwing those faces into strong relief.
   Forgive me, but it was light and darkness again.

MELCHIOR
   Chiaroscuro. Painters do it.

GASPAR
   It was life as art, but by the light, it was life!
   The woman looked startled, as well she might,
   For even in our dusty travelling-clothes
   We three were, what were we, strangers –

MELCHIOR
   Aliens –

BALTHAZAR
            Wizards –

GASPAR
                        First astronomers
   In Nazareth! We calmed her, spoke to her,
   While the baby was all eyes, appearing
   To take it all in, as babies do.

MELCHIOR
   And you were so absorbed I had to remind you
   That new-born children ought to have presents –

GASPAR
   You're right. The whole scene was so strange
   I was caught out of myself. But we gave
   What we could, scrabbling about in our bags –

MELCHIOR
   You found a gold coin, as I remember –

GASPAR
   Yes, and you had a nugget of frankincense
   Which she could burn off and sniff like perfume.

BALTHAZAR
   I handed her a box of balmy myrrh,
   Good for many sicknesses.

MELCHIOR
                              Also
   For embalming the dead.

GASPAR
                                Well well, let be.
   We shall not talk about that, my friends.
   How did the mother react? I can't recall.

BALTHAZAR
   At last she gave a smile, uncertain but thankful,
   Full of grace you might say.

GASPAR
                                I wonder, I wonder –

MELCHIOR
   What?

GASPAR
            I wonder what happened to the boy,
   Assuming he survived in that wretched place,
   That Nazareth –

MELCHIOR
                    Oh it was not so bad.
Peasants survive.

GASPAR
                    But if he was bright,
Supposing he was bright, what would he do?
Who would he talk to – hidebound priests,
Doctors of law, those whose minds are made up?

MELCHIOR
Gaspar, there are different ways of being bright.
You should come to India, we could shock you.

GASPAR
Maybe, maybe. He would be seventeen now.
I can still see those eyes in the light of the cave.

BALTHAZAR
Gentlemen, let us turn our eyes to the stars.

They set up instruments and point to the sky.

Act One Scene One

Nazareth. The family house. Enter JOSEPH *and* MARY, JESUS,
*three of his brothers (*JAMES, JO, *and* SIMON*) and one of his
sisters (*RUTH*). The family are finishing supper.*

JOSEPH
James, so you won't consider joining the business?

JAMES
Father, you know I have absolutely no interest in mortise-joints,
nor have I ever lifted a hod. It's just not me.

JOSEPH
What do you mean it's not me? Who do you think you are? Have
you lilies coming out of your arse?

JAMES
I'd like to teach. I could be good with young people.

JOSEPH
Teaching's not a man's job. Poring over scrolls. Mutter mutter
mutter. Class rise, class sit.

JESUS
But what is a man's job? Is what a man does well not his job?

JOSEPH
Jesus, you ask too many questions. I know you want to defend
your brother, but a father has to think of his sons' future. Builders
will never be unemployed. A father has to guide.

JESUS
Everyone respects a father, and a father has to guide. But does a
father have to command?

JOSEPH
Jesus, I listen to you, because you are not a namby-pamby like

your brother. We have worked together on building sites in Nazareth, in Caesarea, all over, and I know you have a good eye and a strong hand.

JESUS

Even so, I may not be a builder for ever.

JOSEPH

For God's sake, you are good at it! When you marry, you'll be able to keep wife and family in reasonable comfort.

JESUS

I may not marry.

JOSEPH

A bright healthy Jewish boy like you not marry! Mary, speak to him.

MARY

Jesus, sometimes you are hard to understand. What could be better than a happy household, and children being brought up in good order and discipline?

JESUS

Mother, I have nothing against marriage, and when brother Jo holds his wedding festivities in a few weeks time I shall rejoice and drink with him. But just as not everyone is cut out to be a stonemason or a carpenter, not everyone is cut out to be a husband and a father. There are many talents and no one has them all.

JOSEPH

You are beginning to sound like one of those bloody Essenes. They want to snip your bollocks off, to the greater glory of God. Take to the desert, live on dried dates and hot air, talk to the scorpions. God must be hard up for glory. Have you been talking to those fanatics?

JESUS

Father, I will talk to anyone. I am like a vessel waiting for learning, knowledge and truth to be poured in, deep and full.

JOSEPH
  You have not answered my question.

JESUS
  Let me answer you with another question. Do you not trust me? I am not a boy any longer, to be swept along by fads and fancies.

MARY
  Joseph dear, I think that is all you are going to get. Don't force him.

JOSEPH
  Essenes, schmessenes! Searching for the kingdom among the camel-dung! All right, all right, no more. We'll find a bride for Jesus yet.

JESUS (*smiling*)
  The world is wide!

RUTH (*suddenly catching up the earlier part of the conversation*)
  I could carry a hod.

MARY
  Ruth!

JOSEPH
  You're havering, girl.

RUTH
  No I'm not. I am stronger than James. Brother Jo, brother Simon, is that not so?

JO
  I have seen you whacking a ball through a window.

SIMON
  You *almost* threw me once at the wrestling.

JOSEPH
  Simon, you weren't wrestling with your sister!

SIMON

Of course. Doesn't everyone?

JOSEPH

My God, I've got a nest of polymorphous perverts –

JO

Not a bit of it, father. We're a normal lot. Susanna, my bride-to-be, used to climb trees with *her* brothers. You can't say, once a tomboy, always a tomboy.

JESUS

Would the earth collapse if it was true?

RUTH

Jesus, you're on my side! When I think of Judith, and the way she hacked off the head of Holofernes, I can't believe we are going to spend all our days spinning wool.

JOSEPH

That was centuries ago! Primitive stuff! Things have moved on a bit since then.

RUTH

Not for women they haven't. Where are our heroines today? If I wanted to cut off the head of the Roman governor, you would probably stop me.

JOSEPH

Of course I would. Good God, girl, these are terrible thoughts.

RUTH

The Scriptures are full of terrible thoughts. I've been reading them.

JOSEPH

Is that why the dinner is sometimes cold?

MARY

Come now, leave the girl. She's at a difficult age. She helps me very well, but you must give her a little space to think her own thoughts.

JOSEPH

Everyone wants to think their own thoughts! Am I the only one who's not allowed to?

JESUS

Father, you are a fount of thought, and what you say, we hear. Every family is a cauldron of thoughts, and it is better for that cauldron to bubble and seethe openly than for a set of tight lips to store up inward poison.

JAMES

Our brother is in aphoristic mode: where did you pick that one up, Jesus?

JESUS

I didn't. It's my own. Do you not like it?

JAMES

Oh it's all right. But sometimes I get the impression that you are moving away from us. When you talk like that, it's as if you were using your experience of us to give yourself some kind of authority which frankly you have not earned.

JESUS

All right, I am silent. I take it that I am still allowed to use my eyes and my ears. I defended your right not to become a builder. Let me, in return, become whatever it is I have to become.

(*There is a loud knock at the door*)

JOSEPH

Simon boy, see who that is.

(SIMON *opens door, and immediately a Roman* CENTURION *and two* SOLDIERS *stride in, not roughly but with obvious authority.*)

CENTURION (*looking round the assembled company, and consulting a tablet in his hand*)
Sir, you have one more son?

JOSEPH
I have.

CENTURION
Do you know where he is?

JOSEPH
I do not.

CENTURION
We have reason to believe that your son Jude is a member of a sect of Zealots, whose aim is to overthrow, by all means including violent means, what they call the Roman occupation of their country.

JOSEPH
I hear what you say.

CENTURION
You have no further comment?

JOSEPH
Not at this time.

CENTURION (*to* SOLDIERS)
Search the house for weapons.

(*The* SOLDIERS *conduct a hasty and not terribly expert search of the premises. They have done this sort of thing many times before, and know that the Jews are well-trained in concealment. They are philosophical about the Zealots, though their* CENTURION *is not.*)

CENTURION
All right, you appear to be clean. But do not think this is the end of the matter. Rome has an eye that never sleeps.

(CENTURION *and* SOLDIERS *exeunt. The family remain silent
and watchful in case the Romans should suddenly return.
Gradually they relax, and* JOSEPH *asks* RUTH *how her spinning
is doing. She goes to her large basket of wool and spindles,
rummages about in it, smiles, and says 'It is doing very well.'
She holds up half a dozen wool-encased Roman swords.*)

Act One Scene Two

(*Night. A cave, somewhere in Galilee. Enter* JUDE, *the brother of*
JESUS, *his lieutenant* NAHUM, *and a band of* ZEALOTS. *They are
dressed roughly, and could be mistaken for bandits, but they are
all intelligent and have a political agenda.*)

JUDE

That raid on the Roman armoury was highly successful. I con-
gratulate you all. We now have a substantial cache of what we
must be prepared to use, though I hope our movement will also
progress on a popular front of information and propaganda. There
is a huge dim body of silent unawakened support. The time is not
ripe yet for our revolt. Taxes are not deadly, food supply is reasonable. But that will change, and we must prepare ourselves to jump
very quickly when the situation becomes electric. Well-dispersed
activist cells and diligent weapon-training are the key. I think we
are well organized, and we gain friends daily. There is a longing
for liberation. How are things with you, Nahum?

NAHUM

I have started two new cells in the north, and one in the south.
There is an eagerness to engage in decisive action.

JUDE

Yes, and they will see action, but it must be action at the right time
and in the right place. Planning is crucial. The Romans usually

have good intelligence reports; we must have the same. We do not want to be ambushed, or infiltrated, or mown down like beasts. Be vigilant always!

1 ZEALOT

Forgive me, Jude, for asking this question, but is your family – safe, I mean, to be trusted –

JUDE

It is a good question, and I am pretty sure that the answer is Yes. We are a tight-knit family, and we discuss everything openly and at length. My father is, in general, supportive of the civic authority, but he knows and respects my views, criticizing only my acceptance of extreme violence when necessary. The family has mighty squabbles, but it's essentially a loving unit; no one goes in for betrayal. My brother Jesus is the enigmatic one: I know he is sympathetic to the cause, but he never declares himself. He seems to have some hidden agenda of his own.

2 ZEALOT

Have you worked on him?

JUDE

Jesus is too intelligent to be 'worked on'! But yes, we have talked long into the night on the fortunes of the country. He has passionate longings. He might come over to us yet.

NAHUM

Is there any other business? No? I think we should disperse, carefully, in the usual way. The date of our next meeting will be passed round, again in the usual way. Be careful and watchful, all. Our cause is just, and cannot fail. Before we go, let us sing our anthem, 'Now's the time'. (*They stand*) (*All sing*)

> Land of Moses and of David
> Groaning under foreign yoke
> Now's the time for your enslavement
> To be shattered at a stroke.

> Far too long we've suffered meekly
> Roman swords and Roman shields.
> Now's the time for blades of Israel
> To scythe the Romans from our fields.
>
> God will bless our sacrifices.
> Blood will flow and graves will fill.
> Now's the time for zeal and courage
> To plant our flags on Zion hill.

JUDE

> Thank you, gentlemen. Let us give our salute.

> *(They all give the clenched fist salute)*

ALL

> Death to Rome! Death to Rome! Death to Rome!

Act One Scene Three

The garden of JOSEPH's *house. Night is drawing to a close. The starry sky is gradually giving way to dawn as* JESUS *speaks.*

Enter JESUS.

JESUS

> What is it I must do? I ask and ask,
> But all those brilliant and impressive heavens
> Give not one sign or voice or light to help me.
> I have a throbbing purpose that's not clear,
> Waits to be born, waits to gulp down God's air
> Whether in thankfulness or misery
> I do not know. I only know I wait,
> But waiting must be filled with effort, crammed

With thought, with everything I want to know.
No moping, cavilling, dwindling, no despairing!
Everyone born, every animal, has a purpose.
Can only mine – and by God it is strong –
Be hidden? When I watch my brother Jude
I envy his steely assurance, but he's not me
And I'm not him. It is easy to say
'I am what I am', but 'I am what I will be'
Seems not too bold; yes, I believe it.
O there were glimmerings in the synagogue
But not enough, O not enough for life!
Is change not in the air? One week this land
Is quiet, and the next it bursts and buzzes
With rumours. The countryside is roamed
By scruffy Messiahs, dishevelled idiots
Promising the earth to three bored listeners,
Kings of the east, Kings of the west, stark starers
Preaching the end of present society,
Dangling kingdoms indescribable
Whether in this life or the next. Dear God,
It is the worst sin to deceive the people!
And yet there were – the old books tell us – prophets,
And may be so again. We must be sharp and quick
To whip the chaff away, and search for grain.

How beautiful the early morning is.
New things, good things seem possible again.
Angels twitching their robes on our flat roof?
No, it is only mist, so fresh and sparkling
It tears the heart. My father tells me
There is good work in Egypt, they want builders
For a new Roman villa. I shall go.
There are always wonders in Egypt.
My mind can leave its treadmill, and walk free.

Exit.

Act Two Scene One

Egypt. A builder's yard. A new villa is going up, with monumental relics of Egypt's pharaonic past as a backdrop. Midday heat. The workers seek shade for a short break, and something to eat and drink. The workers are MENEMHET, *an Egyptian, and* SHAZ, *a Babylonian. The overseer/contractor,* MARCIUS, *a Roman, is present with them.*

MARCIUS

Well lads, it's beginning to look as if it might be a house.

MENEMHET

Once the foundation has been laid, you can see where you're going.

MARCIUS

Are you quite clear about where the swimming-pool is to go? The owner is very demanding in respect of cleanliness, and he must have his hot and cold baths every day. How is the drainage?

MENEMHET

The baths will be no problem. They will go according to plan. As for drainage: don't forget I am an Egyptian, and we Egyptians have been studying irrigation and drainage for three thousand years!

MARCIUS

I don't question it. The only thing to remember is that the owner is a man of taste, knowledge, and refinement, and he and his family want everything to be just so. He is also a man of wealth, and promises bonuses for anything specially well done. The corollary of this is that any botched or dodgy work – which I am sure will not apply in your case – results in instant dismissal.

SHAZ

Do we have a time-scale for completion? The hours are long, and –

MARCIUS

I am taking on more builders. One of them, in fact, from Palestine, is due here this afternoon. Right: I shall speak to you again at the end of the day.

Exit MARCIUS

MENEMHET *and* SHAZ *resume work*

SHAZ

I hope the new man isn't a weakling. Some of these stones are a bugger to shift.

MENEMHET

It'll be quite a villa, when you add on the garden and the kennels.

SHAZ

Kennels?

MENEMHET

Oh yes, the owner breeds dogs – greyhounds I think.

SHAZ

What d'you suppose a patrician does with his time in a huge conglomeration like this?

MENEMHET

I don't know. Half of the time he'll be soaking in a bath, with slaves scraping his skin clean of all impurities real or imagined. He'll exercise his dogs, and talk to them. His wife will have a kitchen-garden to look after – no rough work, mind. His children will go to the nearest Roman school, and be taught how great Rome is. Maybe he'll write his memoirs. The days will fly.

SHAZ

Will this go on for ever? Egypt was great once. Babylon was great once.

MENEMHET

No it won't. – Hold this stone while I lever it into position: right.

– No it can't. The Romans are very organized, very efficient, but they are not loved. They have so much power that they have become arrogant, and arrogance leads to carelessness. Sooner or later there will be revolts.

SHAZ

The Romans are very good at putting down revolts.

MENEMHET

True. Well. Still. I think there is definitely some crumbling at the edges. And who knows what mad powerful barbarians from the north could swoop down, break the rules of war, and engulf them?

SHAZ

You hope!

MENEMHET

Well, everything has its time. If you had told our supreme pharaoh Rameses the Second that his country would be taken over first by Greeks and then by Italians he would not have understood you, far less believed you. Everything changes.

SHAZ

Anyhow, not before we have topped out our villa. Actually I think this wall looks pretty good. I doubt if we can do much more to that today. The sun will soon be going down. Let's take it easy.

MENEMHET

Not too easy! Our taskmaster will soon be here with his gimlet eyes and his measuring tape!

SHAZ

I suppose you are right. This corner could do with some squaring and refining.

They work a while in silence

Enter JESUS *with stick and knapsack*

JESUS

My name is Jesus. I think you were expecting me on the site.

MENEMHET

Yes of course. Welcome to Egypt. You have come quite a distance, from Palestine?

JESUS

I have. But I had kindness and hospitality on the way.

SHAZ

No bandits? They are everywhere.

JESUS

I'm sure they are. But no, I had a safe journey.

MENEMHET

I am Menemhet, and I am a native of these parts. This is Shaz, who comes from what is left of Babylon.

JESUS

I am glad to meet you. I want to learn about all places and peoples.

MENEMHET

Well, you have come from one occupied country to another.

JESUS

Surely Egypt will always be Egypt. The name is so rich and so resonant –

MENEMHET

Egypt has been a Roman province these forty-five years.

JESUS

Oh, that is nothing! You have forty-five hundred years behind you. Even the Romans did not set Greek fire to the Pyramids.

MENEMHET

I like your enthusiasm. I like enthusiasm in any case. Even Shaz has a little hidden nugget of enthusiasm which he brings out occasionally.

SHAZ

Am I as bad as that?

MENEMHET

As bad, as good. We shall all get on.

Enter MARCIUS

MARCIUS

Evening shadows, men. Is it the end of a good day's work? Let me see . . . yes . . . that is fine . . . pretty straight and tight . . . this corner could still stand some chiselling . . . the work is a little behind schedule, but I see your new helper has arrived. You are Jesus, from Palestine.

JESUS

I am.

MARCIUS

You have excellent references as stonemason and carpenter. You have done work of this kind before?

JESUS

I have, at Caesarea and elsewhere.

MARCIUS

Very good. Menemhet and Shaz will show you the ropes. Can I just say that the owner of the house has high expectations, and knows what he wants. Always be ready to meet his demands.

JESUS

What is the owner's name?

MARCIUS

What do you mean what is the owner's name? That is of no concern to you. You will never be in contact with him. Anthing he

might have to say to the workers he will say through me. You may
see him inspecting the grounds, but he will not speak to you and
you will not speak to him.

JESUS
Why?

MARCIUS
All these questions! Tell me, are you a Jew?

JESUS
I am.

MARCIUS
I knew it. Jews are trouble. Always were and always will be. Let
me say to you very clearly that if you keep your head down and do
the work that is demanded of you, you will go back to Palestine
with a bag full of coins, but if you behave in a provocative or dis-
obedient manner, I assure you that I have the power to punish you,
within the limit of lashes laid down by the law. Do you understand
me?

JESUS
I understand you very well.

MARCIUS
Right then, we know where we stand. Back to your lodgings now,
all of you. I want an early start tomorrow before the sun gets too
hot.

Exit MARCIUS

MENEMHET
Jesus, you should watch your tongue.

SHAZ
He means what he says.

JESUS
So do I mean what I say. I am what I am and I say what I have to
say.

MENEMHET
You are impossible. But we shall stand by you if we can.

SHAZ
Sure.

JESUS
Maybe I shall say nothing, and we shall have a peaceful life.

MENEMHET
Knowing you, I doubt it. But we all live in hope, don't we?

Act Two Scene Two

Several months later. It is a holiday. The Romans allow an annual 'Festival of Egypt', when the native Egyptians celebrate their ancient religion and culture by holding a procession through the streets. Music throughout the procession; both are strange, yet also impressive. The slow, highly decorative procession comprises figures representing Ancient Egyptian life and beliefs: e.g. the sun-god, ATEN, *holding the golden solar disc, cow-horned* ISIS *the divine mother and protectress,* HORUS *the falcon-headed sky-god,* THOTH *the ibis-headed god of scribes and writing,* SET *the god of storms and violence, represented as a swinish, unidentified animal figure. Perhaps also a representative pharaoh and his wife, in full royal gear, followed by a high priest, and people of various trades – fishermen, builders, musicians, huntsmen, potters. The procession ends with dancers, male and female, climaxing in a belly-dancer, naked apart from beads, whose dance is not vulgar but shows an art developed over thousands of years – erotic nevertheless. The small crowd watching the procession includes* MENEMHET, SHAZ, *and* JESUS.

MENEMHET

I bet you never saw that in Nazareth. By Horus, Jesus, you are roused! You have made a tent of your robe!

JESUS (*greatly embarrassed, covering himself with his hand*)

It is true. I am ashamed that the body should have a life of its own. I could not help it.

SHAZ

Why be ashamed? It's the most natural thing in the world. I used to wonder if you were really human, when you never joined in our joky stories about women.

JESUS

Yes, I am human. I am learning what it is to be human. I am learning all the time.

MENEMHET

What did you think of our gods?

JESUS

Do people believe in them?

MENEMHET

Some do; most do not. But we like the procession. You must remember that we are a very ancient people, and we do not want a few Greek philosophers or Roman tax-collectors to cut us off from the Pyramids and the Sphinx and the Book of the Dead.

JESUS

People with animals' heads? You would worship that?

MENEMHET

I might have done, thousands of years ago. No one took a great cleaver and sliced human nature off from animal nature just like that, for ever. I believe your holy books say that man should have dominion over all the animals, to do with as he pleases. If so, that is wrong. Animals have much to teach us. Don't despise the world of nature just because you can read and write and think you have a soul.

JESUS

I don't despise it. But the world was made for man.

MENEMHET

How do you know? You were not there at the time.

JESUS

Do you think it is impossible that I could have been?

MENEMHET

By the gods, you are the strangest stonemason I have ever come across. When you look at me in that way, I can almost believe you.

JESUS (*smiles*)

I must work on that 'almost'.

SHAZ

Let's go. The streets will soon be empty. People follow the procession into the main square, and become exceedingly merry for the rest of the day and night. The gods of Mesopotamia are very different from the gods of Egypt. To me this was a pageant, most colourful, but not involving. Some day, Jesus, you must ask me about Marduk the great creator and Tiamat the terrible she-dragon whom he killed but whose shattered particles became the universe. How does that strike you?

JESUS

Where is Marduk now? Silent, in libraries. Let the dead bury the dead. And let us bury the day by going home and having our supper.

SHAZ

I didn't say I worshipped Marduk.

JESUS

I didn't say you did. Supper.

Act Two Scene Three

The building site. The villa is nearly finished. It is early morning,
before the workers have arrived. Enter the HOUSE-OWNER,
summoning MARCIUS *in order to talk to him.*

MARCIUS
Sir, is everything in order?

HOUSE-OWNER
Almost so, Marcius. You and your men have done a good job.
When I came out here from Rome I wondered if I would ever
settle: the heat, the flies, the sandstorms: it seemed like an exile.
My wife was in tears sometimes. But now when I see the result of
so much labour, I know we are going to be at home. The cool
courtyards, the lattice-work, the fountains, the swimming-pool
which might have been made in Rome itself, the garden attracting
birds already – it is an excellent job, and you were not recom-
mended to me for nothing.

MARCIUS
Sir, if you are pleased, I am rewarded. I hate botched work, on
whatever scale. I think we have given you a livable house, where I
hope you will be happy for many years.

HOUSE-OWNER
There's just one thing. I brought over with me from Rome a large
statue of Jupiter, the father of the gods. It was chipped a bit and
damaged in other ways during the voyage, and I would like to have
it repaired. It belonged to my father and grandfather, and I regard
it as the protective deity of my house and household. It is really a
sacred object to me. The inscription in particular is in dire need of
refreshing and refining. Which of your stonemasons would do the
job?

MARCIUS
Probably Jesus the Palestinian. He has the potential of being a
difficult character, but he has worked steadily here and I have no
complaints. He has a keen eye and his chisel is used to detail.

While they have been speaking, the three craftsmen have entered and are quietly getting on with the finishing touches on the villa.

MARCIUS
Where is the statue? I shall bring it out.

HOUSE-OWNER
It is behind the door on the left, in an alcove.

MARCIUS *carries out the statue, centre stage*

MARCIUS
Jesus, come here for a minute. I have special work for you. I want you to spruce up this statue, which as you see is chipped and cracked and in not very good repair. Pay special attention to the inscription, since at the moment it can only just be read: IUPPITER. REX.DOMINUS.OMNIUM. You can read Latin?

JESUS
I can. JUPITER THE KING, LORD OF ALL.

MARCIUS
Right. How soon can you start?

JESUS
I cannot start. I cannot do it.

MARCIUS
What! Why on earth not? What is to stop you?

JESUS
My conscience. Jupiter is no king, and he is certainly not the lord of all. Only God is king. Only God is lord of all.

MARCIUS
This is ridiculous. It is only a statue. I am not asking you to bow down before it.

JESUS
How else could I repair it?

MARCIUS

Oh what a typically Jewish casuistical reply! Look, Jesus, you are
a hired man and I am your employer. I am asking you to do something which is reasonable and well within the terms of your con-
tract.

JESUS

It is not reasonable to me. That image of a so-called God is redo-
lent of everything that is effete and decadent in your culture.

MARCIUS

Whether it is or not is nothing to the point. I am giving you a simple command, and if you refuse to comply, I have to punish you,
as I once warned you a long time ago. There will be ten lashes,
administered by two men from the garrison.

JESUS

What I have said, I have said.

HOUSE-OWNER (*who has overheard this conversation, and now
comes forward*)

Marcius, let me speak to this man.

MARCIUS (*gruffly, reluctant*)

Jesus, the owner of the house wants a word with you.

HOUSE-OWNER (*to* MARCIUS)

Leave us alone for a few minutes.

Exit MARCIUS, *to some distant part of the site, out of earshot*

HOUSE-OWNER

You are called Jesus, and you are Jewish, from Nazareth?

JESUS

I am. May I ask your name in return. I like to know who I am talking to.

HOUSE-OWNER

Certainly, a fair point. It is Valerius. Tell me why it is impossible
for you to repair the statue.

JESUS

It may be hard to explain to you, because you do not believe that there is only one God, of whom no image can be made. You have a whole pantheon of gods engaged in every kind of dubious or immoral activity; I would be ashamed to list it all. Already many Romans realize this absurdity, and their belief is lukewarm or non-existent. I believe in the God of Abraham and Moses and David – as an educated man you may have heard of them –

HOUSE-OWNER

I have.

JESUS

So Jupiter, Zeus, Marduk, Ra – these are nothing to me, they are human constructs, not real powers –

HOUSE-OWNER

But your god is a human construct too. People write about him, but no one has seen him.

JESUS

No one has seen him, but our knowledge of him evolves. Too many intelligent and truthful prophets have experienced his reality for his existence to be written off as a delusion.

HOUSE-OWNER

You speak almost prophetically yourself. Do you seriously believe that this invisible nameless Palestinian spirit is about to supersede the life-giving Venus and the wise Minerva and the brilliant Apollo and the fearsome Mars?

JESUS

I think you know that is a rhetorical question. I do. I cannot say why.

HOUSE-OWNER

With such certainty behind you, then, where is the harm in repairing a man-made statue?

JESUS

I cannot do it. I would rather see Jupiter as a ruin than as an arrogant head in a shrine.

HOUSE-OWNER
I see I cannot change you. I regret it. You are an interesting person
among so many yes-men and forelock-tuggers here. I cannot com-
mute your sentence; it is the law. But my good wishes go with you,
wherever you find yourself.

JESUS
Valerius, I thank you, and farewell. Tell Marcius I am ready.

HOUSE-OWNER *summons* MARCIUS, *hands* JESUS *over to him, and
exits*

MARCIUS
Jesus, follow me.

MENEMHET
Marcius, be merciful! It is his religion, not his pigheadedness, that
makes him behave this way.

SHAZ
Is it such a fault, to refuse to chip away at a statue?

MARCIUS
You cannot plead for him. The law is in process. Come, Jesus,
quickly.

Act Two Scene Four

Punishment room in the Roman garrison. Two SOLDIERS *strap*
JESUS *to a frame with his arms stretched out. The scene is proleptic
of his final scourging and crucifixion. Dark room, strong light on
the three figures. The* SOLDIERS *whip* JESUS *in turn, five lashes each.*
JESUS *flinches but makes no sound. The* SOLDIERS *count each
stroke. At ten, the scene blacks out.*

Act Two Scene Five

A cell. JESUS *is alone.*

JESUS
    This is pain, bad but not too bad; pain.
    Do I deserve it, God of my fathers?
    Who deserves anything in this life of ours
    When the divine gift of being is life itself?
    We suffer from sin, but goodness does not save us.
    There is nothing, nothing we can demand
    Once we shoot from the womb; the gift is total.
    Why should we crawl about and cry and cringe
    Shouting 'Not me' or 'Unfair' when thousands and thousands
    Roll about with javelins in them or are burned
    At the stake or crucified – dear God
    You let six thousand scream along the Appian Way
    When Spartacus lost his war – I see a world
    That sits upon a cusp of change, waiting –
    Waiting – waiting – for something I cannot see
    But must be some enormous renovation,
    Some revolution, some rousing with a voice
    Of love and not of horror. Can that be?
    I live; scars will heal; I will go back
    To Galilee. I slough another phase
    And hope I still have time to shine anew
    As snakes do, glistening on their pathless way.
    If God wills, there might even be a path.

Act Three Scene One

A few years later. JESUS *is about twenty. Morning in Sepphoris, a sophisticated Greco-Roman city four miles from Nazareth. A pleasant colonnade of shops.* AGATHON, *mid-thirties, director of the municipal theatre, and his sister* HELEN, *an attractive, intelligent woman in her mid-twenties, are slowly strolling along, waiting for* JESUS *who has been invited to see a play ('Antigone' by Sophocles) in the recently refurbished outdoor theatre which he and his father had helped to rebuild.*

HELEN
What will Jesus think of this place now?

AGATHON
That, we shall find out. Sepphoris
Has grown and spread even since he was here,
And what he saw of it then was not much,
Slaving with spades and mallets all day long.

HELEN
Did he walk here from Nazareth?

AGATHON
                                        Of course.
He's fit! He's no slouch! At the moment
He's just dusting himself off, emptying his sandals,
Slipping a little lime drink down –

HELEN
I think we must give him a tour of the city –

AGATHON
Starting with the theatre workshop –

HELEN
                                        Something
He will never have seen before –

AGATHON
                                    Something
  To let a few scales fall from those eyes –

HELEN
  Piercing eyes –

AGATHON
                          Piercing, but he too may be pierced –

HELEN
  We shall open him up –

                          (*they laugh conspiratorially*)

AGATHON
                                But here he comes.

                          Enter JESUS, *with stick and knapsack*

JESUS
  Well now my friends, I am ready for you.

AGATHON
  We are very sorry your father could not make it.

JESUS
  I am too, but he is far from well.

HELEN
  You are in our hands for the whole day –

AGATHON
  And the whole night. You will stay with us?

JESUS
  Thank you, I will. I am much in your debt.

AGATHON
  Right then. Let us go. To the workshop!

Act Three Scene Two

AGATHON's *theatre workshop. Rows of actors' masks, comic,*
tragic, and grotesque. As AGATHON, HELEN, *and* JESUS *approach,*
some of the workshop youths put on masks and prance before the
visitors. It is strange and almost frightening.

AGATHON
What do you think, Jesus? These are hand-crafted,
Superbly made for resonance. This afternoon,
In the amphitheatre, you will hear our actors
Roar through those holes, sing through those slits,
Show you how passive masks can master passion.

JESUS
Something in me does not trust a mask.
What does an actor believe? Nothing.
He is a puppet, he struts with his untruths.

AGATHON
Art has truths, imagination has truths.

JESUS
How can a lying voice deliver truth?
Who is going to put a robe on truth,
A quality robe of many colours?
Truth has a white tunic, that is all.
Truth has no need of megaphone or mask,
She stands and speaks, and she is clearly heard
By those who have ears to hear. Let them hear!

The masked youths mockingly point to their ears

AGATHON
Someday someone will ask you, What is truth?
I hope you know the answer! Never mind,
Let us go forward. There is more to see.

*They come up to a shelf filled with strap-on phalluses, some long
and smooth, some stubby and knobbly, some just monsters which
would be the pride and joy of a modern fetish boutique.*

JESUS
   Good God, these look like – Surely you don't –

AGATHON
   They are, and we do. One of the lads, show us.

*A youth wearing a comic mask quickly straps on an impressive
phallus, grunts through the mask, and thrusts with the phallus.
It is comic and horrifying at the same time. There is a general
ripple of laughter.*

JESUS
   Well, I have heard of Greek civilization –

AGATHON
   Jesus, don't be such a willie-wet-leg.
   You and I both came from one of these.
   We use them in high satiric plays
   Which I wish you could see. You have heard
   Of Aristophanes?

JESUS
                        Never, I am glad to say.

AGATHON
   Oh you have many things to learn. Helen,
   Tell him how tightly buttoned up he is.

HELEN
   It's true, you know. You must let the world in.
   It is not going to destroy you. The reed bends,
   The rod breaks. You think a good man
   Cannot have art, cannot have pleasure?

JESUS
   No, I don't say that, I can't say that.

It's just that – all this is new – my mind
Is whirling, invaded by dervish images –

HELEN (*puts her hand on his arm*)
   So you must let us help you to absorb
   The dervish, dance with him, don't fight him.
   Do you think we would do anything
   To damage someone we're so fond of?

JESUS
   I am learning. I am in your hands. Where next?

AGATHON
   I think a bite to eat. There's a taverna
   Round the corner. Meze, glass of wine,
   Two glasses of wine perhaps. And after that,
   Oh you don't know what lies in wait for you.
   (*to youths in workshop*) Thank you lads, we are moving on now.
   Keep it up – the good work, I mean.

Act Three Scene Three

A narrow, 'discreet' street. Enter AGATHON, HELEN, *and* JESUS.

HELEN
   Is this the most salubrious way to –
   Where are we going?

AGATHON
                        I would say probably not,
   But I want Jesus to at least cast his eye

Over our most expensive brothel. Jesus,
I hope you will not be trying to tell us
There are no brothels in Jerusalem?

JESUS (*sighs*)
I'm sure there are. No doubt there must be.

AGATHON
But perhaps not quite like this. We Greeks
Are not spoilsports. We like to cater. We like
To provide. In these matters of the flesh,
Tastes are – no, not unpredictable,
But varied as the colours of the rose.
We'll just walk past, look in, that's all.

*The house has a low window (unglazed of course) and an open
door. Two of the girls are leaning their bosoms on the sill and
fixing their already beautifully fixed hair. Little lamps inside throw
flickering shadows over an array of objects – whips, dildos, spiked
shoes – and over a couple of impressive bouncers. Soft music plays.
Soft perfumes play. It is a temple of pleasure. What catches the eye
of* JESUS *is the figure of a gorgeous boy of sixteen, lolling in the
doorway; he has eye-shadow and lip-gloss and neatly curled hair.
Like the girls, he is flimsily dressed. He sees* JESUS *looking at him,
and thinks he might have a client.*

BOY
Like what you see?

JESUS (*confused, but curious*)
Yes. No. I mean, how much
Does it cost? Can you make a living here?

BOY
I do extremely well. Fifty for oral,
Hundred for a fuck. I am V.W.E.

JESUS
What is that?

BOY
>   Where have you been living?
>   Very Well Endowed. Do you want a feel?

>   JESUS *makes a swift gingerly pass at his crotch*

JESUS
>   Good God! That must be a strap-on?

BOY (*indignant*)
>   Certainly not. That is real. That is me.

HELEN
>   Jesus, I think we must be moving on.

BOY (*edge of menace in voice*)
>   I always charge twenty for a grope.

JESUS
>   I have no money, I am sorry. My friends
>   Are looking after me today.

BOY
>   I said
>   I always charge twenty for a grope.

HELEN
>   Agathon dear, pay him. These boys
>   Are dangerous. They have their protectors.

>   AGATHON *hands over money, and drags* JESUS *away*

BOY
>   Fucking tourists!

Act Three Scene Four

A huge pillared hall for gaming, gambling, dancing, wrestling,
drinking, and generally rubbing shoulders. A band is playing.
Buzz of conversation, occasional shouts. Enter AGATHON,
HELEN, *and* JESUS.

AGATHON

I will not say this is the *pièce de résistance*.
I hope that will be the play, later
This afternoon, in our splendid amphitheatre.
But here you have Sepphoris set before you.
This is not shepherds driving flocks. Look,
A slight argument, happens all the time.

A game is being played on the floor. Complex lines are marked
out, and pebbles are used as counters.

1 PLAYER

That's a three, not a seven. It wasn't on the line.

2 PLAYER

It fucking was! Have you got eyes or are these just chuckies?

1 PLAYER

I can see through you, anyway. I put good money on this set, and
I'm not going to watch a scabby cheat like you scoop it up.

2 PLAYER

You won't be able to in any case.

He pulls out a knife and stabs the other player in the stomach.
Some friends drag the body off. 2 PLAYER *pockets his winnings.*

AGATHON

Sorry about that, Jesus. This place is not genteel, not at all.

JESUS

Now we shall never know which one was right, shall we?

AGATHON
  Might is right, in this cavern at least.

HELEN
  I see there is a place to prove it. Look –

A rough wrestling-ring has been set up. The BARKER is touting for a match. A flabby, gone-to-seed wrestler is doing his best to look fierce.

BARKER
  Gentlemen – gentlemen – roll up – have a go – who is strong? – who is brave? – you see in front of you the famous Hercules VII, many times champion of this town –

AGATHON
  – in years gone by –

BARKER
  – he will wrestle one straight round, one fall, the usual rules, the winner to receive this magnificent belt –

AGATHON
  – which has seen better days –

BARKER
  – come now, some likely fellow – this young man, how about it sir? (*points to* JESUS)

HELEN
  Jesus, why not? You are very fit, Hercules is a has-been.

AGATHON
  Go on, Jesus. Pin him to the floor. You can do it.

  JESUS, *perhaps emboldened by his recent couple of glasses of wine, accepts the challenge, stands forward.*

JESUS
  I will take him on.

BARKER
Excellent. What is your name?

JESUS
Jesus.

BARKER
Ladies and gentlement, a fine match, Jesus versus Hercules!

> JESUS *strips off. He is well made. His job as construction*
> *worker has kept his muscles in good trim.*

BARKER (*rings bell*)
Gentlemen – grapple!

> *A small crowd has collected, and shouts encouragement or*
> *mockery as the match proceeds. After various feints and slippages*
> *and brief locks, the puffing* HERCULES *begins to feel his age, and*
> JESUS *jumps on him, bears him backwards, straddles him, and*
> *forces both arms to the floor. The crowd claps and whistles. The*
> BARKER *lifts* JESUS*'s arm and puts the belt round his waist.*

HELEN
Splendid! Now you can call yourself Hercules VIII.

JESUS
Perhaps I could find a less pagan name.

HELEN
Oh you are incorrigible! But we are proud of you, aren't we,
Agathon?

AGATHON
Couldn't have done better myself –

HELEN
I should think not!

AGATHON
Jesus, you were great. Once you are clothed and in your right
mind, we have a reward for you.

JESUS *towels himself and dresses. He is surprisingly unfazed by his exertions. He follows* AGATHON *and* HELEN *into a darker corner of the hall where divans and small tables are set out. The three seat themselves on a divan.*

JESUS

Now this is very pleasant. Where is my reward?

AGATHON (*takes a twist of paper from his pocket, unrolls it, and hands* JESUS *something like a tiny square cake*)

Take and eat. This is for the good of your soul. This is from the resin of a divine plant with pointed leaves like stars which Greek medicine has used for thousands of years. But we do not need doctors to enjoy its delights. Take it and eat it. Its effects are swift, and you will have neither hangover nor addiction.

HELEN

Dionysus be with you! You are between two friends who will look after you.

JESUS *swallows the little tablet.*

JESUS*'s hash dream* (JESUS *in spotlight*)

JESUS

I walk forward quickly, my feet hardly touching the ground. I am on a vast plain strewn with boulders, and as I skim across it I kick the boulders into the distance. They are as light as gourds. I come to a very large boulder and put my arms round it. It flies off at great speed with me into the sky. It has strange patches on it, brown and blue. Some of these I recognize, and I think without wondering about it that this is the earth. I can see the Mediterranean Sea, and the narrow straits that lead into the Great Ocean, but there are other huge shadowy masses of both land and sea that mean nothing to me. I am buffeted by loud winds and begin to lose all sense of size and perspective. I am enormous, brushing clouds aside, my boulder bigger than the moon. I am an Egyptian scarab trundling my ball of dung. Night and day flash past. Now the winds have ceased, and I am sitting in a hollow of the plain with a pebble in my hand. It is brown and blue. I have the whole world in my hand. The hollow,

first hard, has become soft. I lie back in it. It is like a divan. There
are voices I recognize. I open my eyes, my hand is empty.

HELEN

Jesus, welcome back. You were twitching like a dog. Whatever it
was you saw, you will soon forget it.

JESUS

Where is my pebble? I have lost the world.

AGATHON

No, you have lost nothing. You have had a little vision, and you
will soon be very relaxed, and ready for our next and last adven-
ture. The theatre is our final port of call, and you must decide
whether this Hall of Games is more or less real than Antigone and
Creon, whose tragedy, written by Sophocles, our actors will present to you. All I ask is that you will not say, It is only a play.

JESUS

I am in your hands. Greek medicine – well!

*The three leave the Hall of Games, and begin to walk towards the
amphitheatre. At a corner they have to pass an old woman sitting
begging in the street with arm outstretched.*

JESUS

Mother, I have no money. My friends will give you something.

AGATHON

No, we have no time. We must not miss the fanfare. She sits here
every day. Come along, quickly.

The old woman, looking at JESUS *in particular, moves her palm
downwards and points at him with straight skinny arm. She fixes
him with a terrible gaze which strikes to his soul. But* JESUS *is
swept off by his friends, and the woman is left sitting like a statue,
as if she had been there from the beginning of time.*

Act Three Scene Five

The garden of AGATHON's *house. Evening. The garden is
beautiful, in the best tradition of Greek culture.* JESUS *and* HELEN
are seated at a small table, for a simple meal.

HELEN

So who was right? Obstinate Antigone
Who defied authority and buried her brother,
Or Creon who wanted law and order
To check the anarchy of individuals?

JESUS

Antigone every time! It doesn't need a feminist
To see that she acted out of common humanity.

HELEN

We shouldn't give Caesar what is due to Caesar?

JESUS

Certainly not. Nothing is due to Caesar
Who is an oppressor all over the world.

HELEN

You are passionate. You were moved by the play.

JESUS

I am. I was. My synapses are flickering
Thirteen to the dozen, I have to rethink
Many things. I am bruised, I have blushes.
Back in Nazareth they will say of me,
He has been through the mincer.

HELEN (*laughs*)

                              So you have!
How would you like Sepphoris as your city?
A royal palace, an acropolis,

A spacious forum, fountains, splendid shops,
Cool colonnades, mosaics, aqueducts,
Plus our famous theatre which you cut from rock – ?

JESUS
– With a few hundred others, yes, I did!
I see it as a capital, the Jerusalem of the north,
And who would not admire its amenities
Of wealth, pleasure, business –

HELEN
– brothels,
Gambling dens, wrestling-booths, hash sessions –

JESUS (*laughs*)
All right! I said I had been through the mincer.
A city is a city. All types arrive there,
Drawn by the magnet of possibility,
Fulfilment, innovation –

HELEN
But not you?
I must say you acquitted yourself well
In our caravanserai today –
The charivari of our caravanserai –
But it is not for you, is that right?

JESUS
Yes, it would be too distracting, too thronged
With things I do not need, would never need.

HELEN
You are hardly a simple country boy.

JESUS
No, I am not a simple country boy.
I know Aramaic, Hebrew, Greek, Latin,
And enough Egyptian to accost the water-seller.
But I am from the country and of the country
And what I am in search of may take me back there.

HELEN

You do not know what you are searching for?

JESUS

No. No. I do not know. But on I go.

HELEN

I have met the most ambitious men
In Galilee, whose busy-ness impressed me
Less than this terrible emptiness of yours.
Is it a thing, a person, a cause, a kingdom?
If it is not in poor plain Nazareth,
And not in rich and fashionable Sepphoris,
Where will your dream find soil to grow in?

JESUS

I am a wanderer, and may remain so.

HELEN

Too much aloneness leads to delusions.
You must not lose friends, family, lovers.

JESUS

Lose some, gain some, my life is open.

HELEN

Before you know it, you will be thirty,
And that is nearly half your span. Me,
I know it! Brother and sister, easy life,
But there's a world out there – I think.

JESUS

You have a fine place here, best of Greek.

HELEN

The way you say that. What is so wrong
With Greek? Aristotle, Homer, Sophocles?
You Jews have something grudging in you, yet
Where is your philosophy, your science, your art?

Do you not want to measure the sun and the moon?
What makes you so afraid of naked statues,
Or even more, of naked youths at play?
The earth, and human beings, and all their fruits
And nothing beyond, unless old Plato's Forms
With their ghastly ghostliness, and who
Believes *that* – can you not say yes to these things?

JESUS

Not Plato, no, but a beyond, yes.
We Jews have immaterial horizons,
And we have God. There are no statues,
Naked or clothed, of God. We are beyond that.
We are into first and last things. Science?
I give you science; others are well ahead.
If it is a fault, we make God all in all.

HELEN

It is a fault, but I will not persuade you.

JESUS

You are a strange woman.

HELEN

                                   I am a woman,
Perhaps that is what is strange. Do you know
You are attractive to women? Others have said it.

JESUS

I had not thought about it.

HELEN

                                   Maybe you should.
Anyhow, do finish the wine. There's the moon
Just rising, poor slender thing. Are you cold?
I think we should go in quite soon. No hurry.
Take the olives with you if you like.
I am always loath to leave a garden at night.
It casts a spell. Do you believe in spells?

She puts her hand on his arm

JESUS

No, I don't, but yes, it does. Shall we go?
You are the best of hosts, and all is good.

HELEN

Come then (*takes his arm as they rise*), I'll show you to your room.

Close together, they go into the house. The garden darkens.
A fountain plays in the stillness. The moon, though thin, is bright.

Act Three Scene Six

On the outskirts of Sepphoris. Morning. JESUS *alone.*

JESUS

Why do I shake? Why am I so troubled?
What is there in a play that can do this?
I am so ignorant. I am shown up.
In the midst of life I find myself in art.
In the midst of art I find myself in life.
I have learned something that does not have clarity.
A world is pressing in on me – Helen,
Agathon, Sepphoris, but then it's Antigone.
That hard bright difficult martyred thing
With a halter, swinging, darkening,
Deep in a cavern of the darkening State.
O she is real! Not more than Helen is real,
But real too in her own word-given way.
I must think more about the power of words.

I must think more about power. Creon,
Like Caesar, has many followers. Some of them
Say 'Yes, my lord' or 'Wisdom itself, my lord',
But those who disagree must find the words
That make defiance general. Is that an art?
Is it an art to become so simple that
Workers in the fields would stop to listen?
It is good to learn, but then to unlearn?
To unroll a fine carpet whose design
Is always vanishing and unrepeated
But beautiful to any honest eye?
Those who have eyes to see, let them see!

Act Four Scene One

A few years later. JESUS *is now about thirty. A rocky desert in Judea. Trees, shrubs, caves. Out of a cave comes the bearded figure of* JOHN THE BAPTIZER, *fastening his belt and looking up at the sky. He is dressed in shaggy animal skins. He looks eccentric, but powerful.*

JOHN B.

Another fine hot gorgeous useless day!
When did a blue sky ever blanket sin?
Up there should be all swarthy spots and slashes
To match the maculate multitudes below.
The vault of heaven, if that is what it is,
Should fester with the fever of the times.
The whole world is on fire with badness,
As the Buddhists say, and by God they are right
In that if nothing else.   I am called
To dowse a little of that evil flame.
I am a voice crying in the wilderness.
I live on the edge of life, I am poor,
I sweat in camel-skins, I crack the locusts
Which nourish me, and filch the wild bees' larder.
I have to be a wild man to be what I am.
I need no stoa, no agora, no amphitheatre.
Men and women come into the wilderness
To see me, hear me, fear me, yes, but hear me,
I have nothing to give but what I say.
– Dear God, where do all these damn ticks come from?

He stretches, scratches, shakes his head.

Enter a CENTURION

CENTURION II

You are John, whom people call the Baptizer?

JOHN B.
You hardly needed to ask.

CENTURION II
                                    I know,
But the forms must be observed. I also know
You have been collecting crowds, here and elsewhere,
And preaching disaffection: do you deny it?

JOHN B.
The only disaffection I have preached
Is with heart's wickedness and wilfulness
In man or woman, or indeed in child.

CENTURION II
Noble, noble. I have heard differently.
I have agents –

JOHN B.
                    spies! –

CENTURION II
                                a dossier –

JOHN B.
                                            lies!

CENTURION II
You prophesy a change in the order of things.
You claim that history, in moment or event,
And if not now, then soon, stands poised
On a great precipice of old and new.
It is the old, you say, which will not do.
I can tell you Rome deals roughly with the new.

JOHN B.
What sort of vague half-strangled threat is this?

CENTURION II
The threat, citizen John, is that we are watching you.
You are under Grade One surveillance.

If anything remotely anti-Roman
Stains your sermonizing, we shall have you.
My own view is that preachers should be licensed
And wear a badge. Well, perhaps that will come.
In the meantime, be careful. We do not like you.

JOHN B.
I do not think I like you too much, Centurion.
You should know me by now, I am unmoved
By menaces. If I have prophecy,
I prophesy. What I have to utter
I utter. Your cocky tramp-tramp empire
Will not be here for ever.

CENTURION II
                                    Nor will you.
In the present, there is law. Obey it.

JOHN B.
I shall obey what I have to obey.

CENTURION II
A Jewish answer! I have no more to say.

Exit CENTURION II

JOHN B. (*sings*)
                    Rome, Rome,
                    March away home.
                    Your gifts and your glory
                    Are only on loan.

                    I've seen the glimmer
                    Of a different throne.
                    I've smelt the spices
                    From shores unknown.

                    All hands on deck.
                    The hawsers groan.

Where is that kingdom
Not made of stone?

I want that kingdom
That kingdom alone.

Act Four Scene Two

On the banks of the Jordan. Afternoon. A CROWD, *from towns
and cities round about, including Jerusalem, has gathered to
hear* JOHN THE BAPTIZER. *He has still to arrive.*

1 CITIZEN

Have you heard him? Isn't he just another of those dotty holy men
traipsing over the countryside these days?

2 CITIZEN

No no, he's different. I listened to him last week in the desert. You
could imagine the very snakes and lizards being hypnotized by his
voice.

3 CITIZEN

Yes, you can't walk away.

1 CITIZEN

But does he take questions?

2 CITIZEN

Yes yes, he does, he relishes questions. I tell you it's a new experience.

1 CITIZEN

But why does he dress in rags? Some people say he smells. Is that
the odour of sanctity?

2 CITIZEN

They are not rags, they are camel-skins. He lives in the world of
nature, by himself, to meditate, to receive messages, to be basic, to
be a lightning-conductor. Would you rather he wore silk and
sprayed himself with Persian perfume?

4 CITIZEN

They say he was once a priest?

2 CITIZEN

Once, once. But it's now, now! He is his own man.

3 CITIZEN

Here he comes, look.

Enter JOHN B. *He stands on a hillock, sweeps a piercing gaze
over the crowd, and speaks.*

JOHN B.

Listen to the voice crying in the wilderness!
This world, this country, you and all of us
Are not in a great state of grace, my friends!
If anyone thinks he is without sin,
If anyone thinks she is without sin,
Do not believe it, O do not believe it!
I only ask you to be sorry for your sins,
To say and to believe that you are heartily sorry,
To enter the terrifying domain of repentance,
To wish to have the bad, which perhaps you love,
Scoured off, washed out, washed strongly away.
Think of how this parched land lurks to lap
The springs and wings and wells and webs of water
That give it life. What would a world be
Without water? I give you water,
I bring you to water, I give you life
Through water. I am the Baptizer.

1 CITIZEN

What's so new about that? Priests wash.
There are purification laws for the Temple.

JOHN B.

   I am not doing it for the Temple!
   Pin your petty rituals back by the ears!
   I am doing it for everyone!
   I am doing it because the distant sound
   Of the thunder of a new age is growing.
   I am here to prepare you for a time
   When perhaps there shall be no temples,
   No priests, but brilliant bands of believers.

2 CITIZEN

   Are you the Messiah?

JOHN B.

                I am not the Messiah,
   But you will soon see someone who might be.
   I am the forerunner, the harbinger, the herald,
   The man of skins and locusts, strange and lawless,
   Under suspicion, under surveillance, even now
   There are those among you who are quietly
   Scribbling and scrabbling my sayings in deadly shorthand.

3 CITIZEN

   When ur we goany kick oot the fuckin Romans?

JOHN B.

   I do not know. I cannot see that day.
   It is not my work. But if you make it yours,
   You will certainly not be condemned by me.
   – But look now how the waters of this great river
   Have been winking and watching and waiting to greet us.
   Come down, good people, throw off your sins,
   Take the sure step, enter the new life.
   You must immerse, you must be drowned, you must
   Rise again and splutter and sparkle and splash
   Like one new born. Come down, and get that life!

Many people come forward to be baptized. We are told it was total immersion, with the candidate naked, but obviously with some arrangements made for modesty. People are not silent, but chatting quietly. It is a good dignified communal occasion, without anything happy-clappy or hysterical. Evening comes on during the baptisms. The powerful, tireless figure of JOHN THE BAPTIZER *becomes a silhouette, broken by flashes of water.*

Act Four Scene Three

Nazareth. The garden of Jesus's parents' house. Enter JESUS *and his brother* JUDE.

JUDE
What's this about you going down to Judea?

JESUS
I have to see this man, this John, this Baptizer.

JUDE
Why? Are there not charlatans enough in Galilee? They line the road and howl their chants, and there's always a large bowl which is not held out for rainwater.

JESUS
If ninety-nine percent were charlatans, there might still be one who has a message that people go a long way to listen to. I think the Baptizer is that one.

JUDE
They are sheep, these followers of his. It is a sheep-dip. They come baaing out, and are free to sin as much as they like, all over again.

JESUS
Won't you think better of us all, brother? Suppose they do really

repent, suppose they do, or some of them, really change their life?
The water is only symbolic, but it may be symbolic of a commitment, a commitment of the heart, of the soul.

JUDE

The heart, the soul! What about the hand, the arm, the voice? This
Baptizer – I know his type, oh I know his type – he wants to see
the tears rolling down your cheeks for some domestic peccadillo,
while you look on indifferently at your country being squeezed and
raped and terrorized by a foreign power. Save the individual soul,
and let the nation go to sleep.

JESUS

You do him an injustice. Rome regards him as a potential troublemaker.

JUDE

Potential, potential, what use is that?

JESUS

I know you are all fiery and bristling in these matters. But consider. The Baptizer foresees some great change, a new phase of
history. It will be social as well as individual. It will not necessarily
be pro-Jewish and anti-Roman and that may be hard for you to
swallow. Hard for *me* to swallow, I may add. You know I have
always had a lot of sympathy with your ideas.

JUDE

You have, you have, I know. It is just that I feel something ominous about this man and what he might do to you. We might lose
you, Jesus. Now that our father is dead, we ought to hold together.
And speaking of family, you remember that Greek woman you met
at Sepphoris?

JESUS

Of course. Helen.

JUDE

Did you know she has a child, a little girl, called Anna?

JESUS

I did not know. I should have kept in touch. How old is she?

JUDE

Oh I don't know. Five or six. Helen still lives with her brother, who is very supportive. They are said to be happy, all three.

JESUS

Anna, a Greek name.

JUDE

Or Latin. Or Hebrew. A good choice for a single parent's child.

JESUS

No one told me. No one told me.

JUDE

Anyhow, there it is. Maybe you will go to see her someday.

JESUS

Maybe I will. Maybe I will.

JUDE

But to get back to the point at issue: you do still mean to meet this Baptizer?

JESUS

I do.

JUDE

There is something black and dangerous in the offing, I can sense it. Don't go.

JESUS

I think I must go. If there is a risk – we are born to take risks. Wish me well, Jude.

JUDE

Of course, of course. You are as obstinate as I am.

Act Four Scene Four

On the banks of the Jordan. A small crowd. JOHN THE BAPTIZER
has just finished baptizing a group, and is drying his hands. JESUS
comes through the crowd and faces JOHN. *It is clear that both
men have great charisma, though in different styles. The people
on shore are curious and respectful.*

JOHN B.

Your name is Jesus, and I knew you would come.

JESUS

John, your fame is great, all through the land.

JOHN B.

I know that we are both marked out, but you
For greater things, more strange, more terrible,
But greater far. I am the first to say this.
Let all who have ears, hear! This is the man
Whose sandal I would scarcely dare to unlatch.
But I knew we were bound to come together.
My mother used to tell me how at the time
She was pregnant with me, your mother came
To visit her; she too was pregnant with you,
And at that news I'm told my unborn limbs
Kicked with joy. These are wonders.
But nature is full of wonders, and will be.

JESUS

Why do you live alone, like a wild man?

JOHN B. (*laughs*)

Because I am a wild man. Look at me!
I needed the basic bone and birth of things,
Uncluttered by clothes, or counting of coins,
Or chase of children, I wanted the sky
And the ages and any lights and perfections
That would come from the mind and be delivered

To the minds of others. Rock and water
(Plus a little honey on my locusts)
Sustained me alone, but I speak to many,
As I speak now to you. What is your desire?

JESUS

To be baptized.

(*The crowd mutter and whisper a little*)

JOHN B.

Jesus, it is rather you
Who should baptize the Baptizer. I
Am what I am, you are what you will be.
You have powers far beyond my reach.

JESUS

I am a man. No one is without sin.
If I say that I am sorry for my sins,
Will you baptize me?

JOHN B.

It is not proper.

JESUS

It is proper. This has to be fulfilled.

JOHN B.

I will baptize you then. The lively water
In this river is only water,
But you will emerge into a new life.

JOHN THE BAPTIZER *takes* JESUS *down to the river, and in sight
of the people baptizes him. As he finishes, there is the sound
of a voice which no one can trace, and which is not particularly
loud or even clear, saying,*
This is my beloved son, in whom I am well pleased.
People in the crowd mutter and talk.

1 CITIZEN

   Is it his father? Is it Joseph? Have you seen Joseph?

2 CITIZEN

   Joseph is dead. He died not long ago.

3 CITIZEN

   It might still be his spirit, loath to leave his family, hovering
   around us like one of those pigeons.

1 CITIZEN

   It is very strange. Are you sure of the words?

2 CITIZEN

   Not really. There were other noises, the crowd breaking up, the
   water splashing. But it *seemed* –

3 CITIZEN

   Whatever it was, let us think about it. These are extraordinary
   times.

(*Exeunt, except* JESUS)

JESUS

   I heard it. They heard it. What was it?
   How do I know it was the voice of God?
   Demons ride the air, everywhere,
   Tempting us with pride and overreaching.
   I must examine myself, must take a scroll
   Out of the Baptizer's book, strip myself down,
   Get myself a desert where the silence
   Will probe the very pith of my desires
   As deep or shallow as they are, as true
   Or false.   God, give me this last step
   To reach the country I was made to reach.
   Hide me in your wilderness a while.

Act Five Scene One

The Judean wilderness. Stony, terrifying landscape. Evening.
Enter SATAN, *who should not be an obviously or crudely sinister*
character. Like JESUS *and* JOHN THE BAPTIZER, *he has his own*
charisma and intelligence, and is capable of a range of thought
and feeling. One is not required, of course, to trust him.

SATAN
  This is one of my favourite desolations.
  Not that I dislike busy throngs, parties,
  Funerals, parliaments, stock exchanges,
  Where there is always business to be had,
  But it is good to stride out of the fray
  At times, and those savage natural scenes
  Attract many a troubled soul, alone,
  Wandering, vulnerable, admirable prey
  For me to talk down into rank despair,
  And after rank despair (*laughs*) there's only hell.
  How I despise those searchers and those waverers!
  Once they meet me, they're ready for the pot
  That seetheth, we are told, for evermore.
  (These images are crude, and if I spelt
  Hell out as it really is, greatest divines
  Would blanch and run run run to prayer.)
  And so this sweet delightful desolation
  Becomes a tempting threshold to damnation.
  Those bluffs and boulders and those black ravines,
  Those shifting shafts of light and crumbling caverns
  Are truly my theatre, and what is played out here
  Raises applause in one place or, if I fail,
  And that's not often, another.
                                        I am waiting
  For a visitor, someone of interest at last.
  I shall stroll about, meditating.
  He is no fool, but well then, I am bright.
  I am Lucifer the Prince of Light.
  Here he is, picking his way through the rocks.

Enter JESUS, *looking gaunt and half-starved*

Jesus of Nazareth, I was expecting you.
We are well met. Do you know who I am?

JESUS

You are the Prince of Darkness, the Father of Lies.
You are the enemy of all mankind.
This unkindly spot seems rightly yours.

SATAN

No spot is rightly mine. Ubiquitous
Is one of my titles. You are a romantic
If you imagine places of gloom and ghastliness
Are my stamping-ground. They may be,
But orgies in the sun, sudden knives in the market
Have netted me a soul or two to fry
(I speak metaphorically of course).

JESUS

For even one soul to be lost to God
Is not a joke.

SATAN

                    Well, you know, that depends.
Millions of souls like sprats go flitting through
God's hands and mine, small beer, small change,
Not bad, not good, are you going to count them?

JESUS

I am. He is. We are. Everyone that lives
Has a soul for angels and devils to wrestle over
If there are such things as angels and devils.

SATAN

If I am not a devil, what am I?

JESUS

I do not know. I know who, not what, you are.

SATAN

    This is beginning to be a conversation.
    My power is almost unimaginable.
    I wonder how much of it you can imagine.
    You have powers, as yet unexercised.
    I think we have a contest. This is fate.

JESUS

    There is no such thing as fate.

SATAN

                         You were fated
    To go to Sepphoris, where you –

JESUS (*a little nonplussed*)

                       I wanted
    To go to Sepphoris –

SATAN

                  but not to meet Helen –
    That was fate, and the Greeks have a word for it.

JESUS

    I take my sins, not fate, to the great last day.

SATAN

    O do not be so quick to talk of sin!
    And do not be so solemn! A little fate
    Is like a little spice from Zanzibar,
    Take, enjoy. It's not in my plan for you,
    Sepphoris, lovely name! What is my plan?
    Let us be more comfortable, and eat.
                    (*They sit*)

The First Temptation

As we sit here in this relentless place
I marvel at your stamina. Hungry
You must be after a week's abstinence.

It is sometimes said that holy ascetics
Regard the desert as their truest home,
Living as simply as will hold body together.
I keep my eye on the Essenes – you know them? –
I thought so – to see if the sin of pride
Will take them to my trap. Only they
Know the true law and obey it. They hide
From the hurly-burly, they hug their virtue.
Calling themselves the Sons of Light, and you,
Jesus, and all your co-Jews, Sons of Darkness
Is a first step to perdition. They will go down.
I am the Son of Light, the only one.

JESUS (*laughs grimly*)
Lucifer died when he was thrown from heaven.
Satan has no light, not a chink, not a spark.

SATAN
A dark lamp may still illuminate,
As you will find. My point though is this:
You are no Essene, no hermit, no purist.
What you are doing in this wilderness
I can only guess. I do not need to guess
That you are ravenously hungry.
Now I have two propositions: first,
I ask you to remember and think seriously
About good John the Baptizer's outburst
When he attacked the crowd for being more-Jewish-than-thou
And told them God could even now
Make better people out of stones than those
Who clung to empty ritual and long robes.
Stones, Jesus! Plenty of them here!
If God can do a golem, make them men,
How easy to make them into loaves of bread.
Shazam. No problem. Crusty and golden,
Whiff of new-baked fragrance. God is great.
I see you are groaning slightly. Say the word.
Be filled.

JESUS
>   Satan, what God can do,
> Could do, will do, is not to be measured.
> I will not make him such a conjuror.
> Any such bread, if it materialized,
> Would plop out fully plump and poisoned
> From the satanic bakeries you control.

SATAN
> Almost a humorous turn of words there,
> Not quite though. We are getting on.
> I come to my second proposition:
> In my theatre I have a great art of illusion
> Which I now exert. My illusions
> Are sometimes more real than life itself.

> *He whistles, gives a loud cry, crashes two rocks together.*
> *A mouth-watering banquet appears.*

> Now if you are truly hungry, reach out,
> Jesus son of your father who was pleased
> With you, perhaps not at this moment.
> Reach, touch, partake. Prod the peach,
> Shake the kebab, tinkle the wine, nothing
> Is genetically modified. Your eyes
> Are sick with longing. Be good to yourself.

JESUS
> If I allowed a crumb or a sip of your offering
> To pass my lips, I would be yours for ever.
> I shall get by on roots and well-water.
> You cannot tempt me. You did try!

SATAN
> Oh, perky. The starved man rolls a jest,
> If not a joint. I am not discouraged.

> *He claps two stones together, and the banquet vanishes*

> We go our separate ways until tomorrow.

JESUS
　If God wills.

SATAN
　　　　　Oh, he will, he will.

Act Five Scene Two

The Second Temptation

JESUS *is perched on the top pinnacle of a huge temple.*
SATAN, *sitting more comfortably on a buttress below him,*
has a broad grin.

SATAN
　I think you are surprised that I could do this.

JESUS
　Nothing Satan does should surprise anyone,
　But yes, I admit you have ingenious powers.

SATAN
　Now that is really grudging. Do you know –

JESUS
　No, but you will tell me – !

SATAN
　　　　　　　　I have shown
　Not a millionth part of my huge powers –

JESUS
　You boast so true to type, it is like a story.

SATAN (*a bit rattled*)
  My present story is a simple one:
  I want you to jump off from the pinnacle
  To test another stereotype, that angels
  Will at once click into active mode,
  Spread wings, and parachute you beautifully
  Down to the startled streets of Jerusalem.
  If you really are the son of your father
  Who refuses to identify himself
  But who was or is well pleased with you,
  Throw yourself off without fear.

JESUS
                                Satan,
  Whether there are or are not angels –
  I have an open mind on that – no jump
  Will be made by me. The great tempter
  Of mankind – is that praise enough for you? –
  Will not tempt me to tempt God. My strength
  Seems fragile, but it is not really so.
  I command you without angels or devils
  To set me down, as you brought me here.

SATAN
  No problem in that. My quiver of resources
  Is never empty. We shall meet again.

Thunder and lightning. The temple disappears, and SATAN *with it.*
JESUS is again in the wilderness. He has tablets, and writes in
them. He groans with hunger. He sleeps.

Act Five Scene Three

The Third Temptation

*A mountain-top and vantage point. Brilliant morning. An
extraordinary panorama of fields and cities, oceans and fortresses,
a patchwork of boundaries and rivers and towers and pyramids,
all glittering in the sun. Enter* SATAN, *shepherding* JESUS *carefully
and respectfully to the highest point.*

SATAN
> You know you are not my easiest temptee,
> But I can read minds. You are ambitious
> (I see you do not deny it). Show gratitude
> To me and mine, and I will give you this –
> Everything your avid eye sweeps over –
> Horizon to horizon, worldly power
> Beyond the tilt of your dreams. Don't tell me
> You have never dreamed of it, a Messiah
> Sitting on a throne, not practising psalms.
> Throne means king. You, King of the Jews!
> Your brother Jude would be your right-hand man.
> All the people, groaning for change, would bless you.
> I have hit the nail on the head, have I not?

JESUS (*after a pause, sighs*)
> Let this be the last and greatest temptation.
> I have thought of what you offer, many times.
> I do not know yet why I reject it.
> What you call fate, what I call God, has plans
> That somehow circumvent Roman and Jew.
> I am feeling towards those plans. A crown
> Would only be a crown of thorns. People,
> Somehow, among them, wandering, speaking,
> 'Of no fixed abode' – is that my kingdom?
> All I know is that my kingdom is not this.
> > (*gestures over landscape*)
> Fold it away, and yourself with it. Now.

SATAN (*bows*)
  You will regret it.

JESUS
                    I regret many things,
  But I shall never crave to own a world,
  Or crack a whip at it, or sit in state
  While beggars pick their sores beside the gate.

SATAN
  So be it, Jesus. This is not the end.

JESUS
  So be it, Satan. Farewell. Fear the end.

  The panorama vanishes, and SATAN *with it.* JESUS *is left in the*
  wilderness, standing very still. Some wild beasts bark, but he
  takes no notice.

JESUS
  Not clear, but clearer than it was, my way.
  I shall end my fast, go back among men.
  Whatever the kingdom is, it is at hand.
  It is as if the black hole left by Satan
  Is filling with strange joy, with light, with spirit,
  And I tap into currents of desire
  That only a new age will satisfy.
  I am the Baptizer not with water
  But with the spirit, human, more than human.
  I set out into far-off mental countries
  Unexplored, and my own country, my own.

A.D.

The Ministry

The Cast
(*in order of appearance*)

KING HEROD ANTIPAS
HERODIAS, wife of Herod
JOHN THE BAPTIZER
CAPTAIN OF THE ROYAL GUARD
COURT POET
SALOME, daughter of Herodias
PETER, disciple of Jesus
SIMON THE ZEALOT, disciple of Jesus
ANDREW, disciple of Jesus
MATTHEW, disciple of Jesus
JOANNA, follower of Jesus
SUSANNA, follower of Jesus
MARY MAGDALENE, follower of Jesus
JESUS of Nazareth
JETHRO, a leading Pharisee
EZRA, a leading Sadducee
REUBEN, a scribe
KOHATH, a spy
NICODEMUS, secret disciple of Jesus
JOSEPH OF ARIMATHEA, secret disciple of Jesus
JUDE, brother of Jesus
NAHUM, a Zealot
A Roman COMMANDANT
CENTURION I
CENTURION II
JUDAS ISCARIOT
MARY, mother of Jesus
ANNA, daughter of Helen
HELEN
The WOMAN TAKEN IN ADULTERY
JUNIUS, Roman interrogator
SATAN

Courtiers, Guards, Wedding Guests, Citizens, Priests,
Zealots, Temple Traders, Singers

The scene is set in Palestine

Act One Scene One

A room in the fortress-palace of KING HEROD ANTIPAS, *at*
Machaerus, near the Dead Sea. He is the son of Herod the Great,
and is the Roman-approved ruler of a large part of Palestine. To
many Jews, he is a lackey of Rome. Luke called him 'that fox'.
Enter HEROD, *his wife* HERODIAS, *and various court officials.*

HEROD
  Who is this man? Do I have to see him?

1 COURTIER
  He is called John the Baptizer, my lord.
  He has a great following among the people.

2 COURTIER
  He is uncouth, but has a great power of words.
  My advice, sir, would be to speak to him.
  It might please the Jews.

HEROD
                              Might please the Jews!
  I am not sitting here in my palace to please the Jews.
  What does he want? I have more things to do.

HERODIAS
  Send him packing, my dear. Baptize, what an idea!

HEROD
  Has he applied for an audience?

1 COURTIER
                              I don't think –

(Commotion and shouting offstage. With guards trying to restrain
him, the burly figure of JOHN THE BAPTIZER *bursts into the room.*
For all his uncourtly appearance, bearded, dressed in animal skins,
he has a powerful presence, and at once addresses the king.)

JOHN B.

Who is this man? Who is this queen?
By the power I have through nature and heaven's grace,
I am here to tell you, King Herod (but not
Herod the Great, your cruel yet remarkable
Father), that your queen is no queen,
That your new wife is no wife, and in brief
That you are living in sin with a relative.

HEROD

What nonsense! The stability of the kingdom
Is soldered by such family connections.

JOHN B.

Stability be damned! Under Jewish law
You cannot marry your brother's wife
As you know full well. Those that get power
Pull a face at such legalities,
But truth will trip them when it is told.

HERODIAS

Who the hell are you to say so?
What synagogue would let you in?
Have savages started reading scrolls?
Man, your clothes are falling off you.

JOHN B.

I am not a rabbi, I am worse than that,
I am a prophet! I keep guard, I speak!

HEROD

You are a fool if you think we bow
To the niceties of some mildewed law.
My wife is mine and she will remain so.
Denunciation is cheap. If you have any threats,
Keep them for the unwashed hordes I'm told
You hypnotize. But just to make sure,
And to remind you the palace is also a fortress,
I'll give you a dungeon to move about in.

– Guards!

(*Enter three or four* GUARDS)

– Chain him, and take him away.

(*The* GUARDS *remove chains and cuffs from their belts and with some effort drag the struggling* BAPTIZER *offstage*)

JOHN B.
I warn you you are under God's eye!

HEROD
Within these castle walls, I am God.

(HEROD *claps his hands. An* ATTENDANT *appears*)

Bring me a white napkin and a bowl.
I like to wash my hands of such unpleasantness.

(*The* ATTENDANT *exits, and returns with water and towel.*
HEROD *washes, ostentatiously*)

HERODIAS
You should have kept the hurt and let it fester.
I for one have business with the Baptizer.

Act One Scene Two

A dungeon in the palace. JOHN THE BAPTIZER *crouches in straw, still chained. Some light comes from a high grating in the wall. He looks up at the grating.*

JOHN B.
That little light, and maybe less to come.
I think I have to feast on those faint rays.
They will give me not much else: water, crusts.
I know these people – they do not love me.

The king has a few slight flickers of grace,
His wife is hard as flint, pitiless.
Will they starve me? Shall I rot here, unseen
While the world shifts and shivers in time's arms?
I never felt as dark as this till now.
I need the wind and air and stars and streams.
I need my dear people, my hesitants
And my enthusiasts, my dunderheads
With sleepy eyes that might just take a gleam,
My children – not my own, as if, as if! –
I kick ball after ball into the net
Of their innocence and they kick back, they laugh,
They shriek, but they will not forget
That wild man with his flapping camel-skins
And words that come – they don't know! – straight from heaven.
– Oh, oh, so much to say and do I had –

(he lifts his arms and clanks his chains)

But now I fear it must be left to others –
To Jesus whom I jauped into the Jordan
To joust with his genius the jurmummle
Of the waters and jump into eternity.
When I think back on that jundy it was like
A jizzen of joy, it makes a jacinth of this jail!
When I am famished, you are my food.
When I am fearful, you are my friend.
When I am finished, you are my phoenix.

(he lies down to sleep, his chains grinding and clanking)

Act One Scene Three

*A banqueting-hall in Herod's palace. Guests are seated at a long
table to celebrate the king's birthday. Musicians are playing quietly
in the background – never loud enough to drown what the guests
are saying.* HEROD *and* HERODIAS *are richly dressed and in jovial
mood. Attentive servants refill glasses. There is a hush of pleasure
and subdued excitement from the guests, who include both Jews and
Romans. Two toasts are called for in succession. The first is from
the* CAPTAIN OF THE ROYAL GUARD:

CAPTAIN

　　Noble friends, honoured guests, it is my pleasant duty as Captain
　　of the Royal Guard to propose a toast to the royal couple whom I
　　serve and protect. You see before you a happy pair, not long joined
　　in matrimony, who can be relied upon to uphold both family
　　virtues and the security of the State. And as we, gathered round
　　this table, are both Jews and Romans, we trust a similar harmony
　　will prevail throughout Palestine, under the wise guidance of King
　　Herod and his beautiful queen. Please join me in standing to drink
　　to King Herod and Queen Herodias.

　　*(All stand and drink. Applause but scarcely an ovation. Some
　　eyebrows are raised, some glances exchanged, but most seem to
　　feel it was at least a diplomatic speech. All sit. The* COURT POET
　　then stands up for the second toast.)

POET

　　As Court Poet, I know you will be glad to hear that I have com-
　　posed a Birthday Ode for the king himself, which I propose to
　　read.

　　　　　　　　(mild groans from guests)

It is quite short.

　　　　　　　　(mild cheers from guests)
　　(he produces scroll, clears his throat, and begins)

Behold, I have aroused my slumbering muse to sing
The virtues of our much sung king
Who was born on this very day
How many years ago I cannot say
But he is in the prime of life
Holding the hand of his lovely wife.

He is the very panther of Palestine,
The gazelle of Galilee, our virile vine.
He floats like a dragon on the Dead Sea.
His nuts fall from the almond-tree.
Long health and a deep purse to our lord and master
And may he never have a disaster.

(*The king laughs and throws some coins to the poet. The guests
stand to drink the toast, and subside with half-ironic cheers and
whistles.*)

HEROD

Dear friends all, on behalf of my wife and myself (*smothered
titter from guests*) I thank you for these loyal toasts which I shall
always treasure. The world is an uncertain place, and we must hold
together as we do at this moment of celebration, Jew and Roman
(*faint smothered hiss from at least one guest*), to further the cause
of peace and order in our society. We are grateful, and we shall
show it.

HERODIAS (*rises*)

Indeed we are grateful, and as a small instant reward to the company I shall ask my beloved daughter Salome, who is an expert
dancer, to perform for us now.

(*Enter* SALOME. *Lights are dimmed except for spotlight on her.
Music. After a pause in which she stands motionless, as if waiting
for inspiration, she begins the dance, which should be beautiful
and elegant but undeniably erotic – perhaps of a 'seven veils'
type, but not too clichéd. The lights come up. The guests are
spellbound, but finally break into enthusiastic applause, led by
the king himself.*)

HEROD
My dear Salome, that was a dance to beat all dances. What can I give you to show my pleasure and my delight? I have coffers of gold and silver. I have jewels – heirlooms. I have silk from China. Not everyone pleases me but you please me. You roll back some dark thoughts. What I have is yours. Confer with your mother, and tell me what it is you want.

(SALOME *and* HERODIAS *go apart and whisper together.*
SALOME *is seen shaking her head, but her mother seizes her and insists: it is something she must do.*)

SALOME
I want the head of John the Baptizer on a platter.

(*There is a gasp of horror from the guests. The queen sits down with a set, terrible, triumphant face. The king is visibly shaken: this is not what he intended. He sees things slipping from his grasp into a dangerous and undefined future. But he cannot go back on the words of his publicly uttered promise.*)

HEROD
Salome, Salome, consider what you are saying. Consider what you are asking for. You cannot really mean it. Think of the fine gifts I can shower you with.

SALOME (*aware of her mother's fixed gaze, answers like an automaton*)
I want the head of John the Baptizer on a platter.

HEROD (*despairing, but caught*)
Guards! You know your duty. Go down to the dungeon, and do what is required.

(*the guards salute and exeunt*)

HERODIAS
Good friends at this table, I want you to understand that in John the Baptizer we are dealing with a thoroughly disaffected and danger-ous demagogue who would be only too happy to disrupt the care-

fully engineered concordat between Jerusalem and Rome. He is a fanatic who veneers his political dissidence with a religious gloss that dazzles all too many simple people of our country. We shall not, my husband and I (*she looks at him sharply*), hand over the keys of life and death to anyone who seeks to usurp our authority; on the contrary, we shall use them. As now.

(*The stunned company are jolted into stifled cries of horror and disgust as the guards return, salute the king and queen, and give a brass platter into the hands of Salome. The shaggy, bloody, jaggedly hacked head of John the Baptizer is shown by Salome to the guests. Herodias smiles. Herod looks grim and drained, but dare not evince any emotion. Spotlight on the platter.*)

Act One Scene Four

A hillside in Galilee. Some of Jesus's disciples and followers are gathered to discuss the new situation presented by the murder of John the Baptizer. Enter PETER *and his brother* ANDREW, JAMES *and his brother* JOHN *(these four all fishermen),* MATTHEW *the tax-collector, and* SIMON *the Zealot. There are also three women:* MARY MAGDALENE, JOANNA, *and* SUSANNA.

PETER

I think you all know that John the Baptizer has been killed by Herod.

SIMON

Brutal beyond words! Peter, why do we suffer this regime?

PETER

That is something we must discuss, Simon, but it is not the only thing we must discuss.

ANDREW

I agree. John the Baptizer, for all his eccentricities, was such a

charismatic figure that he leaves a huge and dangerous gap which
must be filled – and quickly.

PETER

True. I have already heard people lamenting and beating their
breasts and saying they were sheep without a shepherd. As
Andrew says, this cannot go on.

MATTHEW

We can count on only one man. John, without knowing it,
groomed him for the succession. He falls into place, he leads, he is
to be trusted. Jesus is the shepherd for the flock.

SIMON

Matthew, are we quite sure that he is strong enough to resist the
Herods and centurions and torturers of what the Romans call their
province?

MATTHEW

There are strengths and strengths. There are words, as well as
swords. Jesus may be relatively untried, but he already has a
following. He speaks with strange authority. He is the man.

PETER

Do the women agree? Joanna?

JOANNA

That is why I am here. There is no one else. I have come to wander
the roads with you. I have left the comforts of Herod's palace,
where my husband is still the steward. When I told him my intention, he swore at me and hit me, saying that my shame would go
with me for ever and that I was dead to him from that moment. My
companions would be rogues and vagabonds, some married –

PETER (*smiling*)
That's me –

JOANNA
– some not –

ANDREW (*laughs*)
That's me –

JOANNA
– and like every follower of Jesus I would come to a bad end. But here I am, and I am with you in all things.

PETER
For cushions and courtly music I can promise only hard roads and camp-fires. Your sacrifice I take as a noted sign of change and I bless you for it. And Susanna? You are young, are you sure you want to give up so much?

SUSANNA
I am sure. I heard John the Baptizer speak once, in a field like this, and he put iron into my whole soul, which had been timid before. I will go with you and you will not find me wanting.

PETER
And Mary from Magdala: you know Jesus, do you not?

MARY MAG.
I do. We have spoken together, not once but many times. He has lifted me out of very very dark depression. His power is extra-ordinary. I am not an innocent: I have been divorced, and I have had a fraught liaison with a spooky pagan officer in Herod's household – oh yes, Joanna, I too am post-Herod, very post-Herod! – and, or but, I have sloughed off the things of the past and I lay my life, such as it is, into the hands of Jesus who is the future. Count on me.

PETER
I see the man coming, and others with him.

(*Enter* JESUS, *who is now about thirty. He is a man of note: piercing eyes, a healer's hands, a containedness which is like a concealed spring. People would always follow him. Despite the containedness, there is something very physical about him, and one can understand his appeal to both men and women. He is as far as possible from*

the simpering 'gentle Jesus meek and mild' of some later Christian
imagery. He greets the group of disciples, hugging the men and
kissing the women.

JESUS

It is a bleak occasion on which we meet. The Baptizer was my
friend as well as being a beacon for the country.

PETER

That beacon must not be allowed to go out. Will you say a few
words to the brothers and sisters?

JESUS

I will.
I will tell you a story – it is not a parable,
It actually happened, though you may
In your wisdom take it as a parable.
One evening I went out to have supper
At the house of quite a well-known Pharisee.

VOICE FROM CROWD

What were you doing hobnobbing with Pharisees?

JESUS

Is it wrong to accept a polite invitation?

SECOND VOICE

Why do you always answer a question with a question?

JESUS

Am I not a Jew?

THIRD VOICE

Let the man tell his story!

JESUS

Very well. I entered this man's house,
Somewhat hot and dusty after a walk,
Made my salutations in his hallway

Went in and sat with others at the table.
We had not even begun the first course
When a woman crept in from nowhere,
Off the street, evidently a prostitute,
And before anyone was able to stop her
She crouched behind my chair, crying,
Washing my feet with her tears, wiping them
With her long dark hair, anointing them
With a jar of sweet oil she had brought with her.
I asked the woman why she had done this.
'I heard you were here, that's all, I heard you were here.'
Oh you should have seen that Pharisee's indignation!
A sinner! Had she stolen the oil from a client?
What was she doing in such a house as his?
I waited till he simmered down a bit.
'When I arrived,' I said, 'you offered nothing,
Water nor towel nor oil, for the hot feet
Of a traveller, as ancient custom demands.
Perhaps you thought I was not a gentleman?
This woman may not be a lady, but
Whatever sins she has are washed away
With the tears she shed. I have the power
To say this; I say it; it is said.
She saw something that ought to be done,
Something that was not being done,
Something that could be done, and did it.

VOICE FROM THE CROWD
Burn down Herod's palace! Get his head on a platter!

SECOND VOICE
No, his wife's head! She is the bad one.

THIRD VOICE
Scraffle their strong-room, it's hoachin wi dollars!

PETER
Friends, friends, you must stop and think!
Roman revenge is swift and terrible, I've seen it.

SIMON

Peter is right. It would be madness. If you want to see the back of
the Romans, you must prepare, prepare, prepare. Jesus did not say,
You must bomb the bastards out of their basilicas.

VOICE FROM THE CROWD

So what did he say?

JESUS

I said there were things that were not being done, that ought to be
done, and that could be done.

PETER

My friends, you must think, and ponder these words, they were not
spoken lightly. Do not forget John the Baptizer. He did not go running with guns. The things that have to be done may have to be
done inwardly before they can be done outwardly. Things are to
come which are being formed, like the acorn which glistens as it
sends down its roots. Be patient. Be vigilant. Go home now, my
friends. Things have been started which will not go back, I do
assure you of that.

(*The crowd gradually disperses, showing signs of disappointment
and uncertainty but obeying Peter. JESUS is left alone. He climbs
to the top of the hill. It is growing dark, and stars appear. He
gazes at the sky.*)

JESUS

Such brightness in such darkness! Can these
Be worlds like ours, and starry swords be sharpened,
Plots be hatched, and pillows punched for rest?
Empires are not for ever. Stars go out.
Babylon goes down. Rome is broken columns.
How do I know? What are prophets for!
It is no comfort if a second Jerusalem
Is rising from the rocks of the red planet.
A merciless broom will rubbish it too.
My dear Helen used to chide me in Sepphoris
Because I knew so little of the stars

Or any science; I have learned since then.
But life, divine life, what are its chances
If we are free, free to sin, free to kill?
Poison Herodias – that would rejoice many.
A helping hand to get her into hell
Before she takes more heads off? That's not it.
On such a night I look into my soul,
Which like all men's is a darkness, God knows,
But then in spite of pinpoints of light
I see a growing flare, a flash, a diamond,
Jagged, hard-edged, and truly hard to bear,
Baring and boring me to the bone,
A blade of hope that cuts all monstrous things
And casts them like dead flaky worlds away
Although I suffer every word I say.
In such a sky and earth I cry, I pray.

(JESUS *with arms outstretched, then prone, invisible on the hilltop.*
Hold for some moments the brilliant starry darkness.)

Act Two Scene One

A council chamber. Trumpets announce the opening of a session.
Enter Pharisees, Sadducees, Scribes, and various priests and
officials. Enter JETHRO, *a leading Pharisee;* EZRA, *a leading*
Sadducee; and REUBEN, *a Scribe.*

JETHRO

Gentlemen, these are disturbed and disturbing times. What we
have to do, if anything, is not yet clear. I hold no brief for John the
so-called Baptizer – we certainly do not need baptism to add to our
problems – but his murder was, at the least, unwise, and the
manner of it cannot but be inflammatory. There are already signs
of unrest.

EZRA

Thunderclouds gather on the Negev. Owls are shrieking in the
waste places. Order is in jeopardy.

JETHRO

Ezra, I was not talking about nature. Nature is never at rest. There
is such a thing as weather. You Sadducees must loosen your
ancient and conservative robes and consider that the possibility of
change, of real change, is something that has to be thought about.
Society itself changes.

EZRA

Society? Any change that comes from below is an abomination.
You, Jethro, are bound to uphold the Law, just as we are. Therefore to suggest that this august council should bow to a blip in
social arrangements is, if I may use the word, pharasaical. The
Law and the mob are enemies for ever.

JETHRO

I never said we should bow to the mob. I said we should take note
of what might become an escalating situation. Do you want to see
thugs with staves swarming into the temple?

EZRA

That is painful language. In the days when there was a proper aristocracy of councillors, we kept melodrama out of our deliberations.

REUBEN

Gentlemen both, as a Scribe I have to remind you that we have a serious agenda, and we must not lose sight of it.

JETHRO

I agree, Reuben. The killing of John the Baptizer has unleashed a degree of popular discontent which in my view we cannot simply disregard. It may be at bottom a problem for the Romans: the maintenance of public order and discipline. But even in the temple we do not live in a vacuum –

EZRA

Trust a Pharisee to kowtow to the Romans!

REUBEN

Gentlemen, gentlemen. The matter in hand.

JETHRO

As I was saying, before that temple-trotting greybeard interrupted me, we have to recognize a real and not an abstract situation. Rome is the occupying power. Rome will do as Rome wishes to do. We shall watch Rome, as we watch our own people and our own country. Reuben, tell me, is there an actual revolt?

REUBEN

No, there is not, though some wish it. The mantle of John the Baptizer has fallen squarely on the shoulders of Jesus of Nazareth, whom he baptized. Jesus is an enigmatic figure at the moment. He refuses to be pushed into heading a rebellion, but no one knows how firm this is, or indeed what else he can do. He has a growing following of ordinary folk, including women, who go from place to place to hear him speak. He speaks well, as if he had authority. He has a dozen disciples, as he calls them, but there is a hard core of three, and these are the ones that need our vigilance. Peter is the most important, with one reservation which I shall come to. He is a man of action, a strong personality, a born leader. James and John are brothers, and were fishermen, fishing now, as they say, for souls. They are both vigorous minds, but John is the one to watch. He's intelligent, he's a visionary, he's a poet. Peter acts; John writes. John is very close to Jesus, he's called 'the beloved disciple' or 'the disciple whom Jesus loves'.

JETHRO
Isn't that rather odd? Is Jesus – one of those – ?

REUBEN
No no, Jesus is straight. About John, we don't know. It is rumoured that Jesus has a partner somewhere, and a daughter. We have been unable to check this. Our agents, however, have managed to intercept a piece of writing by John, which I think we should all hear. Where is Kohath, our agent?

EZRA
Spy.

REUBEN
Agent.

EZRA
We never needed spies in my day.

JETHRO
Oh come off it, Ezra. Information-gathering is as old as time.

REUBEN
Guard, call for Kohath. He is in the outer room.

(GUARD *calls for* KOHATH. *Enter* KOHATH, *an unprepossessing man, holding a scroll. Despite his rather hangdog looks, he has a good voice, and reads impressively.*)

JETHRO
What is it, Reuben, a manifesto?

REUBEN
  Not exactly. It is almost a poem, almost a psalm, almost a mantra.
  But you must hear it, and then decide. It may only be a fragment.

KOHATH (*holding up scroll*)
  In the beginning was the Word.
  The Word was *with* God, yet the Word *was* God.
  The Word was there in the beginning with God.
  The Word was the one who created the world.
  Nothing was not created by the Word.
  Through him comes all life, now as of old.
  He is the light of the life we hold.
  In every darkness it shines like gold.
  The dark may fight, but its fight is foiled.
  Fighters for light become the children of God.

EZRA
  What is this mumbo-jumbo? Can you imagine anyone in the
  temple opening a scroll and reading words like that?

JETHRO
  It is certainly very strange. It deliberately echoes the book of
  Genesis, where, we are told, God created the heavens and the
  earth, but contradicts it. Apparently there were two of them at
  work. God has a doppelgänger, a sort of ectoplasmic deutero-deity
  whom he projects out of himself and who then goes on to create
  the universe. This is bizarre. As the philosopher said, *Entia non
  sunt multiplicanda praeter necessitatem.*

EZRA
  Translation, for God's sake!

JETHRO
  'Entities should not be multiplied unnecessarily.'

EZRA
  Why do you quote Latin?

JETHRO
  Why not?

EZRA
  And why do you answer a question with another question?

JETHRO
  Am I not a Jew?

REUBEN
  Gentlemen, the point, the point! What are we to make of this disciple, and what are we to make of Jesus of Nazareth?

JETHRO
  Watch them both. I am sure the Romans are doing it, but we have our own reasons. What would happen to the Jewish religion if the idea of this double-headed god began to spread throughout society? Where there are two there might soon be three. Do we want to see polytheism coming back again after all these centuries? God is God, and needs no helper.

REUBEN (*to the spy*)
  Kohath, we thank you. Take this. (*gives money*) We shall pay well for further information.

KOHATH
  I will sir. I like the work. Oh yes.

JETHRO
  The business is concluded. Before we disperse, let us join in a holy song. (*All rise*)

> God is God, and needs no helper.
> God is one and only one.
> We his people are still faithful
> Till time is done, till time is done.
>
> Once a people has been chosen
> They resist all blandishments,
> All false prophets and betrayals,
> Catastrophes and banishments.

Let us keep our sacrifices,
Let the ancient altars smoke.
Let unholy feet be absent
Where God once spoke, where God once spoke.

(*They all file out,* KOHATH *last of all, counting his money. He mocks
the billowing robes ahead of him, tugging and smoothing his own
poor outfit as he prances along.*)

Act Two Scene Two

Night. A quiet place. Enter NICODEMUS *and* JOSEPH OF ARIMATHEA,
two of Jesus's secret disciples. NICODEMUS *is a rabbi who visits
Jesus only at night, and will not openly support him.* JOSEPH OF
ARIMATHEA *is a wealthy Jew who is aware of Jesus's concern for
the poor, and problems with rich men, but who waits patiently for
the time when he can be of help. The two have periodic meetings,
always in secret, where they act as a kind of chorus to the unfolding
events.*

NICODEMUS	The egg has cracked.
JOSEPH A.	The greyhound jumps from its stall.
NICODEMUS	The door is opened. Who is out?
JOSEPH A.	The door is opened. Who is in?
NICODEMUS	The bell rings for school.
JOSEPH A.	Where are the children?
NICODEMUS	They have gone to the hillside.
JOSEPH A.	They are hearing a new lesson.
NICODEMUS	Is the temple dark?
JOSEPH A.	The temple has lit its lamps.
NICODEMUS	Even by day?

JOSEPH A.	By day and by night.
NICODEMUS	Are tongues wagging?
JOSEPH A.	Tongues are wagging, robes are twitching.
NICODEMUS	Hoarse are whispers, beaten are breasts.
JOSEPH A.	Scoured are books, poured are prayers.
NICODEMUS	Are they right to worry?
JOSEPH A.	They are right to worry.
NICODEMUS	He is on the road?
JOSEPH A.	He is on the road.
NICODEMUS	Is it long?
JOSEPH A.	It is not long, but it is hard.
NICODEMUS	Watch after him.
JOSEPH A.	Watch after him.

Act Two Scene Three

An abandoned house on the outskirts of a town. JUDE, *the brother of Jesus, and* NAHUM, *his lieutenant, have gathered their band of* ZEALOTS *for a meeting. A cloaked figure at the door, seemingly the caretaker, is being paid to ensure that they are not disturbed. He bows and pockets the money as they enter. During the scene, he puts his ear to a crack in the wall, listens intently, and takes notes.*

JUDE

As you know, comrades, there is a certain simmering of unrest in these parts, following the murder of John the Baptizer. We must try to capitalize on this unrest, but with great care, since we cannot be sure it is directed against Rome, our enemy. John, if he had lived, might well have supported us, but I assume that he was motivated by religion more than by politics, and religion is what we must be wary of. What do you think, Nahum? Are the people muttering about their salvation, or about the state of the country?

NAHUM

Broadly speaking, they are not politicized. They are angry, but they are confused. They are attaching themselves to a new leader, your brother, Jesus, and although I have absolutely nothing against him, I find him an enigmatic figure, speaking in parables and riddles: a born leader who nevertheless refuses to lead.

JUDE

I agree. You have hit it. I know him well! Because this is so, I think we must have a watching brief at the moment. It is clear to me that we are at the beginning of great events which are getting ready to unfold.

NAHUM

Bit of fatalism about that phrase, Jude. Isn't it our job to coax the flower out of the bud?

JUDE

And so we shall, but not yet openly. There is a new factor. Jesus has collected a dozen disciples to help spread his ideas, and out of that twelve, at least two are Zealots – Simon and Judas.

1 ZEALOT *(laughs)*

Is that the right percentage for the future of Palestine: two for politics and ten for religion!

2 ZEALOT

I think Jesus is a write-off. Mark my words, if we latch ourselves onto the Jesus movement, he will abandon us. His mind is set on what he would call higher things.

3 ZEALOT

Is there anything we can do with Simon and Judas?

JUDE

Not directly, no. Simon truly is a Zealot. I was amused to hear him described the other day as 'a near terrorist'. *(general laughter)* How dreadful! I suppose there *are* those who think we can rid our-selves of the Romans through political dialogue.

2 ZEALOT

Idiots!

JUDE

But anyhow, Simon is now committed to the Jesus movement, and that movement is supposed to be peaceful, even pacifist. The intriguing thing is how Simon was allowed to join them?

NAHUM

To give the group more flexibility, wider appeal, more bite? Make it more sexy, as they say nowadays?

JUDE

If opportunity presents itself, we may get in touch with him, is that agreed? (*general sounds of agreement*) As for Judas, I think not. He has changed tack before, and I do not trust him. He is a bit of a thug. People called him Daggerman. He might be a useful ally in a fight, but that is about all. Let us leave him as a problem for the Jesus movement. Agreed?

ALL

Agreed!

JUDE

And as for Jesus himself, watch well, but no contact. It is true that we need friends as well as enemies. If contact becomes advisable or necessary, I as his brother will make it. That seems fair? (*general mutter of near-agreement*) In the meantime, our first business is to ambush that consignment of weapons coming down to the Romans from Syria. State-of-the-art, I'm told. Our friends in the north are well prepared. Let us wish then success in the usual way. (*All stand and give the clenched fist salute*)

ALL

Death to Rome! Death to Rome! Death to Rome!

(*The Zealots disperse, some of them giving the doorkeeper a tip as they leave. He bows and murmurs thanks.*)

Act Two Scene Four

Same scene. The doorkeeper takes off his cloak and reveals himself as KOHATH, *the temple spy. He gives a little jig, grins, jingles some coins, and speaks.*

KOHATH

How sweet it is to be a secret agent!
Pharisees pay me to suss out Jesus-folk.
Zealots pay me (though the fools don't know it)
To suss out anti-Roman machinations.
It's money all round, money for a song,
Though where and when I'll sing and do my canary
Is still a stone not cast into the river.
O how I love the stepping-stones of power!
I'm on the edge, I'm like an acrobat,
I whistle, put my tongue out at the great,
Keep dusting my cabinet of feet of clay.
I am invulnerable because I believe nothing.
If I should fall, no one cries 'Poor Kohath!'
And that is how I like it. I am shadows,
Footsteps, untraced echoes, I perform
The necessary disasters of the time,
Thankfully thankless in my task.
I bring the wires together. In the flash
You will see messengers running with tiny cracks
They filched from empires, you will see
Palms burnt by pieces of red-hot silver,
Twenty, thirty, dropping them with howls
That please my always open, listening ears.
Money is great but power is better,
Unseen power is best of all.
No one would think of me as a king.
This king goes home to put his notes in order
And study how to bring down – anything.

Act Two Scene Five

Open countryside, with some ruins. JESUS *and* PETER
are sitting on a broken column.

JESUS
  What think you, Peter? Is this the beginning?

PETER
  It is the beginning of the beginning.
  No trumpet will sound, no bell will ring,
  But already you have taken the step of steps
  From which there is no going back, ever.
  You know you have gathered a following –

JESUS
  – of discontented and confused people –

PETER
  Perhaps. But all the readier to be moulded
  By master words or master works, believe me.
  They are yours, they are souls, they are floating vessels
  Eager to be filled, you can scour them,
  Splash them, brim them, they will shine
  In rows like a potter's shop of lamps –

JESUS
  My God, Peter, I can do better than that!
  I am not into filling empty vessels!
  The poorest and the raggedest listener there,
  Suppose he came to gape and gawk, has thoughts,
  Has feelings, has experiences, has desires
  I must engage with. I must wrestle,
  I must convince. Demagogues with buzzwords
  Can get a street looted, a scapegoat
  Tarred and feathered, a Roman chariot torched.
  But that's not it. A cycle of violence
  Fattens crows and ravens, topples columns –

(*he pats the one they are sitting on*)

If that is all I can get people to do
I might as well crawl back into the womb.

PETER
Partly you're right, partly I'm not so sure.
You may despise the blade; others won't.
Look at that broken archway. Think
How troops passed through it, singing, shouting,
Defending, letting blood, shedding their own,
Conscripts? regulars? who knows, but a mass
Of honour, hope, despair, there to the death.
Can you deal with that? Can you get beyond that?

JESUS
Peter, I do not know, but I must try.
If what we are doing is a beginning,
It must be a beginning of something new.
Old wars and desperate defences, of course
I respect them, and the memory of the dead.
But I know there are other dimensions
Waiting to be opened, where arches will not break,
Walls will not fall, and the singing to be heard
Has bartered blood for joy.

(*distant sound of a girl's voice, singing, coming nearer*)

PETER
                                        Coincidence
Obeys you! Or did you know she'd pass this way?

JESUS
I did not know. Sometimes life plays tricks
We are happy with. Call it a blessing.

PETER
Well, let us listen. There is nothing we cannot learn from.
The sun is low. It is a magic time.

*(The girl passes quite near. She is holding a pitcher of water
on her shoulder. She sings.)*

GIRL

>   Goodness of water
>   I carry home.
>   Shadows are lengthening
>   Where I roam.
>
>   Darkness of evening
>   Let me not fear.
>   Spirit of goodness,
>   Guard my ear.
>
>   Water of darkness
>   I guard as I go,
>   Singing my footsteps
>   High and low.
>
>   High among boulders
>   Or low in the sand
>   Homecoming voices
>   Light the land.

Act Three Scene One

A hillside in Galilee. A crowd is collecting, chatting, expectant.
Enter JESUS *and some of his disciples, Jesus taking up a prominent*
position to address the crowd, the disciples standing back. In the
crowd we catch a glimps of KOHATH, *who is there to glean what*
information he can. Jesus lifts his hand to warn the crowd he is
about to speak. He speaks, as scripture tells us, 'as one who had
authority', though no one knows where the authority came from.
He eschews all blandishments like 'Dear friends . . .'

JESUS
   Listen well. I have a story to tell.
   There was a very rich man called Mammon
   Who lived in a mansion of many rooms.
   He dressed in a purple cloak as if he was a king,
   With garments of purest linen under the cloak,
   Ate and drank as if food dropped from heaven,
   And laughed and lolled and snoozed and diced with dice.
   He never seemed to notice at his gate
   A beggar lying there called Eleazar,
   With suppurating sores all over his skin
   So that he could never lie at peace.
   He fed on greasy scraps of bread thrown out
   After Mammon's guests had wiped their hands,
   Their mouths, on those makeshift napkins. Never
   Did he flinch when stray dogs licked his sores.
   – Well now, in course of time they died, those two.
   Mammon got hell and Eleazar got heaven.
   Mammon began to fry and cry and try
   To persuade heaven to allow Eleazar
   Access with his single wet finger-tip
   And lay it on his tongue, his agony.
   What do you think? Heaven said no, no;
   You should have been sorry long long before;
   Now you will be sorry, very sorry, for evermore.

VOICE FROM CROWD
    Is that what you get for being a bit negligent,
    An eternity of pain and punishment?

2 VOICE
    Why did the beggar keep on lying there?
    He must have got more than a few scraps of bread.

3 VOICE
    I think your God hates wealth –

2 VOICE
                         and pleasure –

1 VOICE
                                   and dogs!

JESUS
    I like participation! Listen again.
    Do you know the purpose of a parable?
    You do not know the purpose of a parable!
    I did not say hell was itching and gaping
    For all rich men. I am sure some are good
    And do good works. The question is,
    Is that the best way to run society?
    Exaggerations get the brain-cells going.
    I want you all to think. I once said,
    If your right eye offends you, pluck it out.
    Do you imagine I wanted to hear a multiple splat
    On the pavement of Jerusalem? Give me credit!
    But what did I mean?

1 VOICE
                Guard against temptation.

2 VOICE
    Find your own best means for doing so.

JESUS
    Right, you are with me. A last word on Mammon.

Take a camel. (*someone laughs*) You all know camels –
Big brutes, useful but ungainly, uncooperative.

WOMAN'S VOICE
   I think camels are nice.

JESUS
                     Well, you are lucky.
   But I ask you all to consider this: (*takes needle from lapel*)
   Can you see it, if I flash it in the sun?
   A simple needle with a fine tight eye.
   I want you now to bring that camel up
   And force it through the eye (*laughter*). You can push it
   Like a mule (*he gestures*) or halter it and pull it (*gestures again*)
   You will get hee-haw out of the experiment.
             (*Someone groans like a camel*)
   But still I say to you, it will go through
   Before a rich man ever enters heaven.
   The paradox of the parable is
   That that is not the point. The point is – ?

1 VOICE
   Do we need rich individuals?

JESUS
   And do we? I think not. As the poet says:
   'So distribution should undo excess,
   And each man have enough.'

1 VOICE
                   A commune!

2 VOICE
   A kibbutz!

3 VOICE
           A sect of Essenes!

JESUS
   No, no, and no. What I want is for all.
   It is a renovation of the earth.

(*During these last exchanges, the sky has been going dark.*
PETER *steps forward and speaks.*)

PETER
My friends, I think we should disperse. A storm
Seems to be blowing up. Women and children
Will be soaked. We shall meet again.
Take what has been said back to your homes.
Think, talk, discuss. Nothing is hidden.

KOHATH (*speaking to no one in particular*)
Perhaps it should be. I shall not forget it.

(*Rain begins to sweep across the hill. Distant thunder.*
A general scurry for shelter.)

Act Three Scene Two

A Roman command post. The COMMANDANT *sits at a table,*
fingering documents. Two CENTURIONS *stand at the table.*

COMMANDANT
What are these reports *really* saying? We hear so much about
seething discontent, fanatical prophets, ten-a-penny messiahs,
terrorists with state-of-the-art weapons, superstitious omens, you
would think the Jews were on the point of driving us back across
the Mediterranean. I don't believe it. Do you?

1 CENTURION
We had five soldiers ambushed and killed last week.

2 CENTURION
We know there are cells of Zealots, quite active.

COMMANDANT
Large numbers?

2 CENTURION

No, but they would stop at nothing. We have taken their land.

COMMANDANT

So we have taken many people's lands, that is our destiny! Roman citizenship is greatly prized. An empire brings blessings and opportunities. Why is it always the Jews who want to kick against the pricks, to use their own foul phrase.

1 CENTURION

I think by pricks they mean goads, sir.

COMMANDANT

Damn pedant! Who said centurions should be educated?

1 CENTURION

The Jews have upset you, sir.

COMMANDANT

Of course the Jews have upset me. The Jews are always upsetting me. I have a job to do and I am trying to do it. Who is this Jesus of Nazareth who has started to hold open-air meetings and harangue the gullible provincials? Is there any harm in him? Any danger in that quarter?

1 CENTURION

He is not armed, and he does not preach rebellion, according to my information.

COMMANDANT

A religious nut?

1 CENTURION

Religious, certainly. I am not so sure about the nut.

COMMANDANT

What about his followers? I'm told he has a group, a band of disciples. Could there be a nucleus of something antisocial, anti-Rome? You say he is not armed, but perhaps he has links with

those who are? He has, or had, a brother who is on our books and
on the run. Name of (*shuffles papers*) Jude. Unreconstructed
Zealot if ever there was one. Are they in contact?

1 CENTURION
We have no such evidence.

COMMANDANT
Look into it. Those Jews are clannish and devious.

2 CENTURION
The country swarms with informers. Sooner or later we shall hear
what we want to hear.

COMMANDANT
Sooner rather than later, I hope. And do not forget that informers
(a) are not always to be trusted and (b) have to be carefully paid,
for an underpaid informer is like a scorned woman – hell has no
fury, etc.

2 CENTURION
Money is no problem.

COMMANDANT
I cannot do much more when everything is so vague. Keep good
watch. That is all at the moment. Be in touch.

1 CENTURION
Sir.

2 CENTURION
Sir.

Act Three Scene Three

A cheap rented room in Capernaum, a town where Jesus made few converts. Enter two of his disciples, SIMON THE ZEALOT *and* JUDAS ISCARIOT. *They are drinking wine and speaking more freely than they normally would.*

SIMON

Jesus fairly lambasted the good folk out there today. Sometimes I wonder about him, Judas. He has spasms of anger which I'm sure he would justify but which seem to be well over the top and are probably counterproductive. What had Capernaum done that had to be denounced as if it was a cauldron of vices?

JUDAS

Nothing, Simon! Some people there had criticized Jesus for not starving himself like some ascetic Essene of the desert – he actually eats meat and slurps wine! Oh, and his friends and disciples are not classy, they include tax-collectors and women who may or may not be virtuous. Poor douce Capernaum was looking for a prophet and found a man.

SIMON

And the man turned on them like a rottweiler. What was it he said: 'On the day of judgement it will be more tolerable for the land of Sodom than for you.' How can he believe that that sort of fire and brimstone rhetoric will make people mend their ways?

JUDAS

It is a threat, and no one accepts it has any other truth. Some timid souls may be made unhappy, but the robust will go on their way. How does he know what will happen on the day of judgement, assuming there is such a thing. He will not be around!

SIMON

Actually, he says he will. It is part of his strangeness, his extravagance, his *hubris* as the Greeks would say. He claims that he was there at the beginning and will be there at the end. I have heard him.

JUDAS

You believe him?

SIMON

How could anyone believe that?

(*they pour more wine*)

JUDAS

Jesus talks about his ministry, and says it has only just begun. But where it will go is the great question. You and I have ideas on that score. Are we using him, or is he using us? He knows you are a Zealot, working for the liberation of Palestine. He knows I am too, though not with the clarity of intention you have. So what is the game? Is he running with the hare and the hounds? Will he ever declare himself? I am not the most patient of men.

SIMON

I must say your position is even more curious than mine. You are our treasurer – treasurer of a group that preaches poverty! I know you are good with money, but you won't make much of that in Galilee. I could ask, What is *your* game?

JUDAS

I like money. There may be chances, there may be openings. Even Zealots need money. Keep in with me.

SIMON

When I look at those shoulders of yours, Judas, I think I had better. I can see you as a club bouncer, pocketing backhanders as well as your wages. But here we are in a better life, is that not so? Walking by the shore, conversing, casting nets, persuading multitudes – if we cannot bend some of those circumstances to our will, we are a poor advertisement for the new Palestine.

JUDAS

And what is the new Palestine: praying, scolding, denouncing? Even the Romans must welcome such a confederacy of dunces. The earth gapes for majesty, riches, power. Is it only the miserably squabbling, self-deceived Jews who are doomed never to attain these things? When I think of the dazzling spires of Solomon's temple, and the petty berating by Jesus of some bungling burghers, I despair at our fall from grace and greatness.

SIMON (*shakes an empty bottle; his speech is now very slightly slurred*)
Strong words, Judas, but I share them. If this Jesus, this leader, this prophet, this shaman fails to deliver on the high promises he has made – a kingdom, thrones to sit on, powers to judge – far stronger than the judges of old – if all this is allowed to slip away into the sand, we shall shed him like a shrivelled snakeskin, and be the better for it.

JUDAS
We shall boot him like an empty wine-cask into the lake of Gennesaret, where the fish can have him. What's the Greek for fish? (*they laugh together, their hands on each other's shoulders*)

Act Three Scene Four

By the lake of Gennesaret. Fishermen with boats. A crowd is collecting. JESUS *speaks from a boat where he is standing with one or two of his disciples, including* PETER.

JESUS
Listen well. I am speaking to you from the water,
The element I was immersed in by John the Baptizer
And the element which on this earth gives life.
I will not baptize you with water
But with the spirit: immerse yourselves
In the glint and glance of waves that crash
Into the mind; lie open; I will wash you!
Misapprehensions, conventional wisdom
Must be washed away.

A VOICE

How? Tell us how?

JESUS

A story to help you. A man had two sons.
The younger asked for his inheritance,
Went travelling abroad, lived like a lord,
Shekels spilling from every pocket,
Crowds of hangers-on, leeches, advisers,
Good-time girls, milking him eventually dry.
He became a pig-herder, envying the snouts
Their mash. At starvation point
He decided to go back to his father
In full repentance, expecting contumely.
But his father rejoiced, put robes on him,
Ordered a feast, with wine, with dancing.
How do you think the elder brother felt
Who had stayed working hard at home?
Oh he was bitter, refused to join in.
Was goodness to be neglected, badness rewarded?
His father said, 'To find what was lost,
To have the occasion of forgiveness of sin,
Refreshes the spirit like a summer shower.
I love you no less, as time will show.'
But the elder brother was not convinced.

A VOICE

Neither he should be! Where's the moral?

2 VOICE

The younger brother made a total balls of it.

3 VOICE

Confess, and the slate's wiped clean, is that it?

PETER (*steps forward*)

It is difficult, because it is new thinking.
This is not what you hear in the temple.
Scribes and Pharisees want the Law,

We want more than the Law. Elder brother
Does his work, fulfils his quota, pares his nails,
Keeps his nose clean, observes the rituals –
What a complacent pious berk he is!
Do you see that? Jesus may or may not
Wash his hands before dinner but by God
He washes his soul. We are into change.
The book is great, but we don't do everything by the book!

VOICE (*probably from a Pharisee*)
Would you say you were dangerous? *I* would.

PETER
The things that are valuable are dangerous.
You and we are on the knife-edge of time.
Nothing that is expected is to be expected.
We want to stir you up: we *will* stir you up!

(*The boat sails away, leaving the crowd in some turmoil, people arguing passionately with their neighbours, with much gesturing and some shouting. If Jesus wants interaction, he has got it.*)

Act Three Scene Five

Roman command post as in Scene Two. COMMANDANT *and two* CENTURIONS *as before. A* SOLDIER *enters.*

SOLDIER
Sir, there is a man wants to see you. Bit of a scruff, but he says he has some important information.

COMMANDANT
We have no shortage of 'important information' which usually turns out to be rubbish. As the occupying power, we are fair game for hoaxers. Never mind, bring him in.

(SOLDIER *exits, and returns with* KOHATH)

COMMANDANT (*to soldier*)

Stay just outside the door, in case of trouble.   (SOLDIER *exits*)
(*to* KOHATH) You have something to tell me? What is your name?

KOHATH

Kohath, sir.

COMMANDANT

Are you a Jew?

KOHATH

I am. I come from an old family which has fallen on hard times. I
would dress more appropriately if I had the means.

COMMANDANT

Violins please! I think I know your type.

KOHATH

Sir, I am not a type. I am Kohath.

COMMANDANT

Spirited beggar, eh? Why should a Jew want to help the Romans?

KOHATH

I have nothing against the Romans. I do not necessarily want to
help you, but I do want to help myself. I am told you pay well for
reliable information.

COMMANDANT

Reliable is the operative word. If I like your story, I shall (*takes
chinking bag of coins from a drawer*) give you half just now, and
the other half when the story is proved. My two centurions will
study your body language, such as it is (*laughs*).

KOHATH (*riled but controlled*)

A shipment of arms is coming down from Syria in a week's time,
is that not the case? (COMMANDANT *nods*) There is a narrow pass

twenty miles south of Sidon. A band of Zealots has made precise plans to attack the convoy there. You have time to ambush the ambushers.

COMMANDANT

Good news, if true. From the amount of unrest around, it sounds very probable. We shall take steps. If their plans and our plans materialize and coincide, you will have done Rome a service. Take this now (*gives money*) and be ready to receive the other half if all is as you say.

KOHATH (*bowing*)

I thank you. You will find I am a truthful reporter.

COMMANDANT (*calling*)

Soldier! Escort the gentleman out.   (SOLDIER *exits with* KOHATH)

1 CENTURION

'You will find I am a truthful reporter' – slimy chancer!

COMMANDANT

We must make use of whatever is offered. If he turns out to be a liar, we have ways of making him sorry for it.

2 CENTURION

His story did seem to hold together. And we shall certainly not sing dirges over dead Zealots. But I wonder what the ordinary Jew thinks of it all.

COMMANDANT

I am not interested in the mental processes of the ordinary Jew. We have a military situation. We have a political situation. We do not have a psychological situation.

1 CENTURION

Still, it is important to study your enemy.

2 CENTURION

Since last week, I find myself in that study.

1 CENTURION
How come?

COMMANDANT
I hope you have not been conducting snap polls in the street.

2 CENTURION
No, but it was in the street that something happened. You know my son has been very ill.

COMMANDANT
Yes, and we were sorry to hear it.

2 CENTURION
Our doctor tried everything, but he got worse and worse. It was a fever, a sort of shivering half-paralysis, dreadful to watch. The doctor wrote down P.U.O. on his tablet.

COMMANDANT
'Pyrexia of Unknown Origin', I know it well. Half my troops have been felled in this cursed country.

2 CENTURION
Well, when I was in town, on my way to the chemist, I passed the Nazarene preacher Jesus, and on a sudden impulse – I cannot explain it – asked him to help my son. He stopped, and those extra-ordinary eyes of his looked straight at me. 'Do you think I can?' he asked. I said simply, 'Yes.' 'He will get better from this moment,' said Jesus, and walked on. When I got home, my son was sitting up in bed, eating soup my wife had made for him. He was calm, the fever had gone. My wife was in tears – of happiness – when I embraced her. So what happened? What would magician Virgil say? What would philosopher Lucretius say? Are we in another world now?

COMMANDANT
Fevers come and go. Coincidence has a very long arm. I am delighted at your luck, but luck it was.

1 CENTURION
  Curing by remote control is for fables. Thank your stars, not the
  Nazarene. Your son was born under a good one.

2 CENTURION
  It is very strange.

COMMANDANT
  Do not think about it.

2 CENTURION
  But I do. I do.

Act Four Scene One

*Jerusalem. The temple courtyard. A busy scene of traders and
money-changers. Much chaffering and chattering and clink of
coins. Without warning, a disruptive band bursts on the scene.*
JESUS *is in front like an avenging angel, brandishing and cracking
a whip and crying 'Out! Out! Get out from the temple!' His little
group of followers (who are not his disciples) wear masks and
carry either staves or swords, and they make a menacing swoop,
overturning tables and chairs, though there is no bloodshed.
They are a sort of disciplined ruffians or vigilantes whom Jesus
has gathered for this purpose. The amazed and scared traders
fall back and scurry around, though some are defiant, and scuffles
break out.*

1 TRADER

What the hell is going on? We have been trading here for years.
We are not doing anything illegal.

JESUS

Your disgusting trade may be legal, but as from now you will pur-
sue it somewhere else. Even within sight of the temple there are
beggars and homeless people lying in alleys and doorways, while
you make a mint for yourselves by sharp dealing, and there are
usurers among you who are forcing money to make money, an
obscenity and against nature.

2 TRADER

Anyway, who are you? Who are you to tell us how to do our job?

JESUS

I am Jesus of Nazareth, and if you have not heard of me yet, you
will from now on.

*(Priests and officers emerge from the temple and try to restore
order. Jesus, who has made his point and wants to avoid
unnecessary violence, begins to negotiate.)*

TEMPLE PRIEST
Stop this mêlée at once! It is disgraceful! The temple precincts are used for the decent conduct of essential temple business.

JESUS
Do you think it is decent conduct for traders and money-men to haggle their inflated prices while a poor widow puts her penny in the collection-box and sees it swallowed up in the grand robes of scribes and priests like yourself?

TEMPLE PRIEST
Money is needed for temple upkeep. Animals for sacrifice have to be examined and purchased. This is normal.

JESUS
O great god of normality! If the normal is wrong, you must change it. 'You must change your life,' as the poet said. As for the upkeep of the temple, there will come a time when rats and lizards will forage among its ruins.

TEMPLE PRIEST
The temple is to the glory of God.

JESUS
God is not glorified through megalomaniac physical structures if the poor are gnawing on crusts and the innocent are paying bribes to get justice. The only temples you need are the ones that enfold your brain at the top of your head and allow it to work on improving the state of man and woman. I am the son of man, and therefore I say that to you.

TEMPLE PRIEST
Whatever else you may be, you are clearly a troublemaker, and you may be sure that the temple will take careful note of everything you say from this time forward.

JESUS
That is excellent. Perhaps they will learn something. But in the meantime, can we agree that I and my friends will not carry out

any further troublemaking in your courtyard if you guarantee that the scum, I am sorry, the merchants and money-changers will not be allowed to return.

TEMPLE PRIEST
This has to be confirmed at a higher level, but I think you can take it that a deal will be struck.

(*Jesus motions to his vigilantes to leave, and they all exit together. One of the band gives a huge final kick to the overturned box of coins on the floor. The jingling is like a celebration of the defeat of the traders, who have disappeared. The priests and officials go back into the temple, whispering and gesticulating. They have a new problem.*)

Act Four Scene Two

A dark grove, with frosty starlight. Enter the two secret disciples, NICODEMUS *and* JOSEPH OF ARIMATHEA.

NICODEMUS   Things progress.
JOSEPH A.   Things must not go back.
NICODEMUS   The moon hides.
JOSEPH A.   Or not.
NICODEMUS   The stars blaze.
JOSEPH A.   Or hide.
NICODEMUS   Actions are being taken.
JOSEPH A.   Actions that displease.
NICODEMUS   He is doing as well as telling?
JOSEPH A.   He will be noted, he will be marked.
NICODEMUS   His mother is in the house, sewing, baking, waiting.
JOSEPH A.   Where is his father?
NICODEMUS   Deep in the earth.
JOSEPH A.   Does he speak of him?
NICODEMUS   Not all secrets are out.

JOSEPH A.	But still he goes about.
NICODEMUS	With a rout?
JOSEPH A.	And sometimes a shout!
NICODEMUS	But mothers will be grieving.
JOSEPH A.	Snakes will be crawling.
NICODEMUS	People will be healed.
JOSEPH A.	People will be killed.
NICODEMUS	That the word may be heard.
JOSEPH A.	And the word will be heard.
NICODEMUS	Wrap up, it is cold.
JOSEPH A.	Turn your face to the east!
NICODEMUS	We shall meet in good time.
JOSEPH A.	We shall meet in good time.

Act Four Scene Three

A room in the house of MARY, *Jesus's mother. She lives alone,
now that Joseph is dead and her family have dispersed.* JESUS
sees her when he can, but she also has visits from HELEN, *the
woman Jesus met in Sepphoris, and her daughter* ANNA, *now
a girl of about ten. All four are sitting at a table, having just
finished a simple meal.*

MARY

You know it is a blessing to me to see you all. Life can be lonely
at times. I used to grieve that there had been no wedding for my
daugher-in-law, but you, Helen, have been like a daughter to me,
you make nothing of those three miles between our towns. And
Anna is a delight. She is growing into a fine young lady. Did you
enjoy those cakes, my dear? I made them just for you.

ANNA

Yes I did, thank you, grandma.

HELEN

You mustn't spoil her. My brother is bad enough! He adores her.

MARY

I am so glad that the three of you are happy. Is Agathon still busy in the theatre?

HELEN

Oh yes. He is working on *The Oresteia.*

MARY

I don't know it.

HELEN

No, of course. It is three connected plays, very remarkable but quite a challenge even for the most experienced director.

MARY

Jesus, you saw a play in Sepphoris, did you not?

JESUS

Yes, mother. Greek tragedy was totally new to me, but I must admit that although it had gods instead of God, it held me, it gripped me, a new experience. And that is where I met Helen – another new experience –

HELEN (*smiling*)

– which I hope you don't regret –

JESUS

Never. Some people have problems with it. Either I should have a big motherly Jewish wife pouring chicken soup into me every day, or I should button myself up like an anchorite and say no to the flesh. But I am my own man. On the one hand, I have a mission, where I have to be alone; on the other hand, women are important to me, and indeed are a part of that mission. I only wish you had told me, from the start, about Anna (*he takes Anna to him and gives her a squeeze*). I had to catch up. I had many things to catch up.

HELEN

I should have told you. I did not want it to be a great burden to you.

JESUS

    Love is no burden. If I am a much absent father, I think Anna knows why. You have told her?

HELEN

    Of course. She is bright, and understands.

JESUS

    You know I shall be in danger? Not yet, but it will come. You know this, mother?

MARY

    My son, I am an old Jewish woman who has seen many bad things and will no doubt see more. I put my trust in God.

JESUS

    I must go now. There is a meeting of the disciples. I will come again as soon as I can.

MARY

    God bless you, son. Be careful.

      (JESUS *kisses and embraces* MARY, HELEN, *and* ANNA. MARY
          beckons ANNA *to sit on the floor beside her*)

    You are not too old to hear a story, my dear?

ANNA

    Oh no, grandma. I love your stories. I love all stories.

HELEN (*smiling*)

    We Greeks have plenty of strange tales too. She will be like an encyclopaedia.

MARY

    Well then, I shall begin at the beginning, because there is no better place to start. In the beginning . . .

      (*gradual fade of sight and sound till we are left in darkness*)

Act Four Scene Four

The Roman command post. COMMANDANT *and two* CENTURIONS
*as before. A certain buzz and excitement. Soldiers are entering
and leaving, some with notes and documents.*

COMMANDANT

By Jupiter, this is the best news we have had for months. Kohath
came up trumps. The convoy from Syria was beautifully ambushed
by the Zealots, and then they were beautifully ambushed by us.
How many men did we lose?

1 CENTURION

Four, sir, and seven wounded.

COMMANDANT

Not bad. And the others?

2 CENTURION

About half the Zealots were killed. Some scattered into the hills
and escaped – we shall no doubt see those ones again.

1 CENTURION

But most important: we caught their ringleader, wounded in one
leg but otherwise unharmed. We have sent him straight to Headquarters for interrogation. Name of Jude. Brother of the preacher
Jesus the Nazarene.

COMMANDANT

Aha! And will he sing? He must have much to tell us. I can see us
beginning to crack this so-called uprising. Keep me informed,
immediately, of even the slightest development. Can we do anything about this Jesus? We must think. Send my personal com-
mendation to the troops who broke the ambush. I shall visit the
wounded myself. Oh, and that ghastly Kohath: he is sure to come
back sometime to see whether it is 'Mission Accomplished' –
unless he knows already, he's such a slinky slyboots. When he
comes, if I'm not there, give him his pieces of silver.

1 CENTURION
  Shall we have a jug of wine, sir?

COMMANDANT
  Excellent idea.

(2 CENTURION *goes to cupboard and brings out a bottle and glasses.*
He pours, and they all stand up for a toast, which mimics the toast
of the Zealots, though they do not know that. Instead of the
clenched fist salute they give the Roman salute.)

ALL
  Rome for ever! Rome for ever! Rome for ever!

COMMANDANT
  Our little anthem, gentlemen.

ALL (*sing*)
> From Scythis to Iberia
> From Africa to Gaul,
> We beat the dark barbarians
> Who curse us as they fall.
>
> Their curses have no power
> To stop is in our tracks.
> The eagles of our legions
> Hack their fleeing backs.
>
> The banners of the Empire
> Fly higher, wider still,
> From foggy British beaches
> To the top of Zion hill.
>
> From foggy British beaches
> To the top of Zion hill.

(*The three men give a hurrah and crash their glasses against*
the wall.)

Act Four Scene Five

A public square. People strolling about, enjoying the sunshine.
JESUS *is present with one or two disciples. Suddenly a rough path is*
thrown open through the crowd as a woman is dragged into the
centre by SCRIBES *and* PHARISEES. *She does not struggle but is in a*
wretched state, her hair awry and her clothes tugged about and in
some disorder, her face bent down as if in shame. She is left
crouching near where JESUS, PETER, *and* JOHN *are standing.*

1 SCRIBE
    Jesus, the woman you see in this sorry state
    Has broken her marriage vows, she is a sinner,
    An adultress, caught in the very act –

2 SCRIBE
    In flagrante delicto, as the Romans say,
    With a young man, her husband being out
    Pursuing his business. Her feeble defence
    Was that this husband no longer loved her,
    A defence unrecognized by law –

1 SCRIBE
    So what do you say, as teacher and preacher,
    Do we stone the sinner to death, as usual?

    (*points to a pile of large rough stones kept in readiness for such*
                                executions)

PETER (*intimately, to* JESUS)
    This is a trick. They are trying to catch you.
    They would do anything to bring charges against you.
    Rome has forbidden capital punishment
    To be carried out by Jews, but if you recommend
    Laxity, you break the moral law
    And the Pharisees will pounce upon you.

JOHN
    Machinations all the way. Be careful.

(JESUS, *before replying, bends down and writes with his finger on the ground. The priests, who are facing him, cannot read it, but some bystanders, behind Jesus, can.*)

1 BYSTANDER
What is he writing? Can you see it?

2 BYSTANDER
It looks like a single word: HYPOCRISY.

1 SCRIBE
Jesus, we put a question to you.

2 SCRIBE
We take it that you do have an answer.

JESUS (*straightens up, and speaks*)
Any one of you that is without sin
May lift up the first stone and throw it.
                              (*He bends again and writes*)

1 BYSTANDER
What is it this time? Is it different?

2 BYSTANDER
Yes it's two words: LEGALISM and CRUELTY.

JESUS
I said, Stone her if you have no sin.

(*The prosecutors melt away gradually, one by one, muttering, until the woman is left by herself, facing Jesus.*)

JESUS (*now standing*)
Woman, where are they? Where are your accusers?
Has none of those fine men dared to condemn you?

WOMAN
No one, sir.

JESUS

                    Nor do I condemn you.
Take up your life, but leave that sin behind.

(The woman, in tears, bends, kisses his hand, and runs away.)

PETER

Brilliant. The Pharisees have no comeback.

JOHN

Unless they say, He's loose on family values.
They can spread a bad word about that.

PETER

They'll spread a hundred bad words anyhow.
But people will begin to think. That's good.
Mice are at the old scrolls in their box.

JESUS

In the meantime, let us make ourselves scarce.
I have a sense, though not a fear, of pursuit.
Crowds are fine, but so is lying low.
I have a mind to burn some midnight oil
Thinking of where we are, where going,
What obstacles we can expect, setbacks
To thole, words to spread and words silent,
What enemies to watch, good or bad,
And one by name, our Adversary
Thought to be irrepressible, perhaps,
But ancient in danger and in purpose,
Satan, who keeps looking at the world
Like the last jewel his dark cupboard needs.

Take different ways. Tomorrow we shall talk.

Act Four Scene Six

Roman army headquarters in Galilee. Officers, clerks, documents.
The Chief Interrogator, JUNIUS, *is about to examine* JUDE, *who*
stands in chains before him, with roughly bandaged leg.

JUNIUS
  You were caught red-handed at the Syrian ambush, is that true?

JUDE
  It is.

JUNIUS
  You had personally killed some Roman soldiers?

JUDE
  I had.

JUNIUS
  And you encouraged others to do the same?

JUDE
  I did.

JUNIUS
  How many others?

JUDE
  That I cannot tell you.

JUNIUS
  Will not tell me?

JUDE
  Will not tell you.

JUNIUS
  Very well. We know that some of them escaped and are still at

large. I understand your chief lieutenant may have been among
them. It is important for us to track down these people. What we
want from you is the names of the chief members of your cell of
activists.

JUDE (*is silent*)

JUNIUS (*gesturing to soldier*)
  Help him to speak. (*the soldier hits him hard with the flat of his
  sword.* JUDE *cries out.*) Ah, you have found your tongue. I want
  half a dozen names.

JUDE
  You will get none from me.

JUNIUS
  Make things easier for yourself. Some of your punishment can be
  remitted if you cooperate. We already have some information from
  other sources, not necessarily to be trusted. Our aim is to act
  quickly. I repeat my question: who are your main collaborators?

JUDE
  Do you really believe I would tell you? What sort of agitators
  would we be if we grassed on each other? We are like a band of
  brothers, and our whole aim is to sweep you and your legions into
  the sea, if not by ourselves, then by those who will follow after us
  and will keep the torch burning. You are not rulers, you are occu-
  piers. You cannot send roots down into Palestinian earth. The time
  will come when your empire, already over-extended, will crack
  and slip and crumble and allow the waiting, patient (or not so
  patient) native shoots to push through again and flourish. If I could
  see that I would die happy.

JUNIUS
  You will not see it, and I very much doubt that you will die happy.
  (*to* SOLDIER) Encourage him. (SOLDIER *strikes him again, harder.
  This time* JUDE, *though he shakes, does not cry out.*) I see you are
  a stubborn fellow. But let me ask you (*hoping to catch him off
  guard*), is one of your leaders called Nahum? (JUDE *does not even
  blink or change colour*)

JUDE

I have never heard that name.

JUNIUS

We are getting nowhere. I think polite questions are nearing the end of their usefulness. Take him into the inner chamber.

(GUARDS *hustle* JUDE *through a door into what in plain language is a torture-chamber. We do not see what is happening, but we hear thumps, groans, and eventually screams. There is silence, and the* GUARDS *emerge.*)

1 GUARD

We could get nothing out of him. He was one very determined man.

JUNIUS
Was?

2 GUARD

He will not speak again. What shall we do with the body?

JUNIUS

Leave it just now. It requires thought. I will give instructions. I have to admire the desperation which can make anyone willing to suffer into an extremity like that. However, my admiration will not stop me from ensuring that his death may be useful to us, as his life was not. *Oderint dum metuant*, as the proverb says. Let them hate me as much as they like, so long as they hold me in fear. – Gentlemen, the session is over. We shall of course redouble our efforts to trace and catch the other criminals. Thank you for attending.

Act Four Scene Seven

Outside the house of MARY, *mother of Jesus, in Nazareth.*
Two Roman SOLDIERS, *carrying a heavy sack between them,*
stop at the door and knock. After a moment, MARY *opens the*
door and looks at them questioningly.

1 SOLDIER
  Is this the house of widow Mary?

MARY
  It is.

2 SOLDIER
  We have something for you. Compliments of military headquarters.
  (*They up-end the sack, and let the mutilated body of* JUDE *roll out*
  at the feet of MARY. *They stride off quickly.*)

MARY
  Jude! Oh Jude, Jude! What have they done?

Act Five Scene One

The Judean wilderness. Enter SATAN, *gliding between the rocks
as if he had just emerged from the bowels of the earth. He is in
thoughtful mood.*

SATAN

I like to think of this as crisis country.
He always walks here when he is disturbed.
We are due to meet again, quite soon.
Oh I have many things to say to him,
And so much has changed since we talked before.
Temptation is a lily of the valley,
A rose of Sharon, it makes me leap like a roe
On the high tops. That's enough of that.
But when I think to land the biggest fish,
And none is bigger than this one, I find
Even a nosing of the line, far less a tug,
Sends me into raptures of expectation.
I have a gorgeously black battery
Of instruments, from bludgeons to microprobes,
With which I break, break down, break right down
All the sophistications of resistance.
Even the divine power I wrestle with
To the end of time can have a shock, a jolt,
A useful shudder, when the wilderness
Becomes the testing-ground its ground suggests.

(*enter* JESUS)

I love it when I hear that step; I know it.
He is a troubled man, that Nazarene.
A little luck and I shall have him.
– Jesus, we meet again. I might say I am sorry
For your brother's death, but that would be a lie.

JESUS

Where's the problem? You are the Father of Lies.

SATAN

In this case my main aim is to suggest
How you may benefit from the killing of Jude.

JESUS

I am aware I must not lose my cool
Which would play into your monstrous hands.

SATAN

Well then. I insert first this thought:
Here is your brother felled by Roman thugs,
And in a most cruel manner at that.
He was close; you shared many of his ideas.
He died as an outstanding patriot,
Giving his life for a free Palestine.
You may frown, but you cannot disagree.
I move to a simple two words: avenge him.
Revenge may be a kind of wild justice,
As the philosopher said, but justice it is.
The people will be with you: a hero, a defender.
Make yourself the Zealot you almost are.
Night, and a knife: get the interrogator.

(SATAN *enacts the assassination*)

JESUS

You might have tempted me before I knew
What I was here to do. I understand
That the act would please many. I am here
Not to please many, but to challenge many.
I am not an hour-glass to be turned over.
Give me an angry crowd. What shall I say?
Love your enemies, bless those that curse you,
Do good to those that hate you. If you're struck
On one cheek, hold out the other also.
If your coat is taken, offer the shirt as well.

SATAN

I am your enemy. Do you love me?

JESUS

Would I be talking to you, if not?

SATAN

A weirder reply I have never heard.

JESUS (*gives brief snort or laugh*)

I am glad I can still surprise you. Tempt away.

SATAN

Since you are not man enough to avenge your brother –

(JESUS *shows signs of irritation*)

My second suggestion is: a permanent retreat.
Get yourself to some isolated spot,
Not quite as savage as this, perhaps,
Become a holy hermit, a sainted sage,
Study the stars, write a few Dead Sea Scrolls,
Cut yourself off from the stupid multitude,
Prepare for some perfection of the spirit
Untainted by dispute or disappointment.
Oh I could help you – what a pair we'd make
In rags and bare feet, chewing solemn berries!

JESUS

Satan, if you were not the Prince of Darkness
You could write fiction and sell it too.
Never will you see me abandon the crowds.
I live and die for all who will listen.
The scorpion, the raven, and the snake
Are God's creatures, but I leave them here
Happily unvisited by philosophers.

SATAN

Do I detect a note of wit? Admit
We are made for each other. Your grief,
Where is it now? I seem to have restored you
To your bizarre, footloose normality.
Little thanks do I get for it.

JESUS
>   Nor will.
> God knows if I am footloose; I hope not.
> But I am off now to complete my task.
> I tell you what you know. If you repented,
> I could tell you – oh, much much more.
> I am now the tempter. I know the score.

SATAN
> When I repent, the worlds will be no more.

> (*Exeunt, separately*)

Act Five Scene Two

The council chamber as in Act Two. Pharisees, Sadducees, Scribes, priests and officials. JETHRO *the Pharisee,* EZRA *the Sadducee,* REUBEN *the Scribe, as before.*

JETHRO
> The last time we met, gentlemen, was to discuss John the Baptizer. This time it is Jude the Zealot. Both are dead, but both leave problems. Jude was slaughtered by Romans, which you might say does not affect us. Let them take any backlash that comes up. But Jude was the brother of Jesus the Nazarene, and by all accounts quite close to him. How will *he* react? Ezra?

EZRA
> He is not one of us. He is a wild card. Some even say he is mad.

JETHRO
> I don't agree. More and more he seems to be becoming the crucial factor in the whole situation, and I want to know more about him. What does he stand for? What does he want? Reuben, you are a Scribe, you should know.

REUBEN

No one, Jethro, will give you a straight answer to that. On the one hand, he can be violent, as when he turfed the traders out of the temple. And it wasn't a moment of anger, it was carefully planned, a touch of Jude in him obviously. On the other hand, he is a healer, and a very remarkable one. Sick people queue up to see him. He lays on hands, his eyes are possibly hypnotic, he speaks in certain ways, and clearly he has medical knowledge, perhaps gained in Egypt. This gives rise to magic stories of how he can raise the dead, and he is surrounded by an army of the credulous, which he tries to keep at bay.

JETHRO

And his teaching? Is he against us or for us?

REUBEN

He is a free spirit, an iconoclast. He says the Sabbath was made for man, not man for the Sabbath. If the need arises, he uses it like any other day.

EZRA

Disgusting!

REUBEN

He talks about his father as if his father was actually God.

JETHRO

Well, we are all children of God. We are a chosen people. God is the father of each of us.

REUBEN

Yes, but he sometimes seems to mean it not as a metaphor but as a fact. That Joseph was not really his father at all, that God popped in before him, and Mary delivered what can only be called a man-god or a god-man.

EZRA

Rank blasphemy! Even Moses never claimed to be a god.

JETHRO

I agree this is serious. This gives us another lever. If we cannot prove that he is politically dangerous, a Zealot, an enemy of the state, we may be able to bring a blasphemy charge against him.

REUBEN

Do we want to?

EZRA

'Do we want to?' Good God!

REUBEN

Think about it. He is a great healer. He has followers.

JETHRO

Followers shmollowers! What did he call us – and we are only human, we feel these things – what did he call this august assembly? Generation of vipers; blind guides; hypocrites; whited sepulchres. Are we to act tender-hearted towards such a foulmouth? Let the sick heal themselves, or find another doctor.

EZRA

Even a Pharisee can sometimes hit the nail on the head. We concur.

REUBEN

Is it generally agreed that we have a double-pronged weapon to deploy, if the situation warrants it: either Jesus is a wrecker of the public peace, or he is a spreader of blasphemous ideas?

VOICES (*murmuring agreement*)

JETHRO

I should stress that we are not at that situation yet. Many things have to be taken into account, not least what Rome is thinking. In the meantime – watch, listen, take notes, report. I want to have the fullest possible picture of how events unfold during the next weeks, or even months. Is there any other business?

1 VOICE

Do we compensate the traders who lost either business or goods
when Jesus and his ruffians ransacked the temple?

JETHRO

We do not. Business is business. Let them grit their teeth and stop
girning.

2 VOICE

You sound as if Jesus was right.

JETHRO

Not at all. But in this life you take the rough with the smooth. How
do you think we Jews have survived?

(*A bell rings out. Time for all to disperse.*)

Act Five Scene Three

A cellar. Enter NAHUM, *former lieutenant to* JUDE, *and now
leader of the remnant of Zealots.*

NAHUM

The easy life, not ours, never to be.
The horror of a secret burial
At dead of night, the hasty muffled spade,
A mother in a black cloak, like a statue,
Not weeping, past weeping, proud,
And in the absence of ceremony
That most moving of all salutes,
The few, his comrades, hands on hearts
At the edge of the terrible dark earth
In silence, only a moment, standing there.
O Jude, it is not given to forget you.
Continuing, you with us, like a flag

Invisible to others' eyes, we go
Wherever freedom beckons, like an arm
Signalling weakly from under stones
Thrown by oppression, and we shall break
The stones apart and gently pull that life
Into the sun, as you would have done,
Jude, mentor, leader, dear companion.

The struggle never ends, nor should it end,
As long as grim injustice stalks the ground.
At the encounter I shall still be found.

Act Five Scene Four

*A room in a house used by Jesus and his disciples. Evening.
Only* JESUS *and* JOHN *the 'beloved disciple' are present.*

JESUS
Ah, John, what crowds today! And they demand,
They plead, they argue, they tug my robe,
Ask me to touch them, fight each other
In the scramble to get a crumb of cure,
A drop of salvation, a whiff of mystery.
Some are good and some are not so good,
I can tell, it's not too difficult.
There are semi-tourists, or for all I know
Real tourists, greedy for souvenirs.
And there are some so shy and self-effacing
I have to search them out to reassure them.
I am doctor, teacher, priest, psychologist
And would be, but for Peter, policeman too.
Sometimes I think, Too much! but that's not true.
My reward, though, is to be here with you.

JOHN
We do not often have such conversation.

There is much to say. It is a dangerous time.
Events pile up, relentless, ominous.
Are we in any kind of control?

JESUS

It is often said that God controls.
Man proposes, God disposes, you know?
But that won't do. Maybe our free will
Is given, but at least we have it.
I am still doing what I want to do.

JOHN

I worry if it is self-destruction.
You have powerful enemies now,
Both Roman and Jew. It is a lonely furrow.

JESUS

God knows I plough it straight.

JOHN

                                    You do.
But you make difficulties for yourself.
Some of your sayings may come back to haunt you.

JESUS

Such as?

JOHN

                    Let me quote from memory:
'I have not come to bring peace to the earth,
But a sword, to set a man against his father,
A daughter against her mother; your enemies
Will be the members of your own household.'
Jesus, these thoughts have a hellish potential.

JESUS

By 'sword' I don't mean a sharp-edged iron thing.
It's a figure of speech. Surely you see that.

JOHN

But if you set a man against his father
It may lead to a sharp-edged iron thing.
Think of how people use words. Think
There might be armies using sharp-edged iron,
Wars, massacres, in the name of Jesus.
I have visions of whole fields of blood,
God's ravens picking dead eyes from God's children –

JESUS

Hold on. I know you are a poet,
But I have never set an army out
And never will. What others may do –

JOHN

– you might be held responsible for.
Suppose your words are written down –

JESUS

They will be! You will do it! I know! –

JOHN

Suppose they become a sort of holy scripture,
Everything *everything* may be acted on –

JESUS

Keep the reference to the sword: I want it.
Risks are better than mumbles and slumbers.
I can't imagine massacres in my name.

JOHN

There will be.

JESUS

Light a lamp. It's getting dark.

(JOHN *lights an oil lamp in the semi-darkness*)

Good God, John, that's a Roman lamp!

JOHN
'I shall set lamp against lamp', eh?

JESUS
John, John, none of my other disciples
Could talk to me as you do, free, fresh, piercing,
Opening and closing the dark places of the heart.
My beloved disciple, with whom I am well pleased.

JOHN
Jesus, that's blasphemy!

JESUS
Not a bit of it.
If I cannot say such things, who can?
Anyhow, what is love? Let us leave massacres
And talk about love. My mother, Helen, Anna,
The kingdom of God, though I cannot define it,
These I love. And you love – men, am I right?

JOHN
You are.

JESUS
I always thought so. To me, it is fine,
But you must know there are some Pharisees
Who would vote to stone you tomorrow.
It must be difficult, being that way?

JOHN
It is, it was, it always will be, Jesus.
But we survive. You know, there is in love
A great strength; by it, indeed, we live.
And love is love, whatever flesh it inhabits.

JESUS
Another lamp, I think. It is really dark.
Some good Palestinian pottery this time, please!
        (JOHN *searches for and lights a fine large lamp*)
Now that's a lamp! It's like a moon. You know

The moon and stars are bright in Palestine.
Look up at them from the wilderness
And they are like a script, a coded message
We are being asked to read. In the beginning
There was something; before that there was nothing.
That moment – a moment or an age, who knows –
Surely showed the power of love. Love
Is generous, overflows, wants to create,
Cannot be satisfied with darkness and silence.
This is something the Greeks with all their wisdom
Are blind to, that God, not gods, and not *a* god
Wanted fullness where there was emptiness,
Wanted the gift he was bursting with
To roll out and light up and sing and shout –

JOHN
With suffering and death in the small print? –

JESUS
Yes, yes. He never promised ease. But think:
You are a fisherman: you catch a fish:
It cannot cry, but oh how it squirms and twists
In its desire not to be nothing!
The very presence of life is love.
The sparrow in the summer dust is love.
The great leviathans embrace with love.
The cedars of Lebanon are broad with love.
The snows of Hermon shine and melt with love.
The sun that warms us is a furnace of love.
If God so loved the universe, we too
Should love it, and our neighbour as ourself.

JOHN
I will say nothing against that.
Let us see what this universe is like.
      (*they open the door, and stand staring up at the stars*)

A.D.

The Execution

The Cast
(*in order of appearance*)

NICODEMUS, secret disciple of Jesus
JOSEPH OF ARIMATHEA, secret disciple of Jesus
THE WOMAN OF SAMARIA
JESUS OF NAZARETH
JUDAS, disciple of Jesus
PETER, disciple of Jesus
JOHN, disciple of Jesus
JETHRO, a leading Pharisee
REUBEN, a scribe
EZRA, a leading Sadducee
KOHATH, a spy
A Roman COMMANDANT
CENTURION I
CENTURION II
SIMON, disciple of Jesus
MARY MAGDALENE
DRUNK MAN
MAD PROPHET
CAIAPHAS, Jewish high priest
ANDREW, disciple of Jesus
JAMES, disciple of Jesus
SATAN
MARY, mother of Jesus
HELEN
PONTIUS PILATE
PROCULA, wife of Pilate
The Three Magi (GASPAR, MELCHIOR, BALTHAZAR)

Citizens, Soldiers, Children, Policemen, Witnesses, Officials, Priests, Bandits

The scene is set in Palestine and Persia

Act One Scene One

Evening. A quiet place. Enter NICODEMUS *and*
JOSEPH OF ARIMATHEA, *secret disciples of Jesus.*

NICODEMUS	The darkness gathers.
JOSEPH A.	There are many voices.
NICODEMUS	Voices and torches.
JOSEPH A.	Torches and shouts.
NICODEMUS	Can you see the good and the bad?
JOSEPH A.	The good and the bad are linked together;
	They strike sparks off each other.
NICODEMUS	Fireflies in the cave of change.
JOSEPH A.	Great temples have no fireflies.
NICODEMUS	Great temples are not great;
	Cracks are eating them.
JOSEPH A.	Priests are eating them.
NICODEMUS	Though they do not think so.
JOSEPH A.	Is there a kingdom?
NICODEMUS	There is a kingdom.
JOSEPH A.	Who talks of it?
NICODEMUS	The man is known.
JOSEPH A.	Known and unknown.
NICODEMUS	He will have darkness.
JOSEPH A.	Darkness and pain.
NICODEMUS	Not to be measured.
JOSEPH A.	But not to be lost, whatever the cost.
NICODEMUS	Black is the water.
JOSEPH A.	The bud is in mud.
NICODEMUS	The lily makes for light.
JOSEPH A.	As if there was no night.
NICODEMUS	Far to go?
JOSEPH A.	Not far to go.
NICODEMUS	We must be ready.
JOSEPH A.	We will be ready.

Act One Scene Two

*At a well in Samaria, outside the city of Shechem. It is midday,
and hot.* JESUS, *dusty and travel-stained, is resting beside the well.
His disciples have gone to the city to buy provisions. Enter the*
WOMAN OF SAMARIA, *a good-looking woman of the world, some
would say 'bold'. She is carrying a water-jar to get water from
the well.*

WOMAN S.
Sir, you are not from these parts, I think?

JESUS
I have travelled up from Judea
On my way to Galilee. It is quite a step.
I rest here halfway, in your country.

WOMAN S.
My country? Would the Romans know the distinction?

JESUS
Of course they would, not on their maps
But in their minds. What is Samaria
Other than a stubborn splinter from the stock,
Something that never gels or assimilates.

WOMAN S.
So why are you engaging me in conversation?

JESUS
I am thirsty. I want some of your water.

WOMAN S. (*laughs*)
So we are sometimes useful, we Samaritans,
Is that it? Sir, you are not speaking to a slave.

JESUS
No, I am speaking to a human being.

I am tired, I am thirsty, I am hungry.
The water in the well is not Samaritan,
Nor is it Jewish. When you draw some,
It would refresh me beyond measure.

WOMAN S. (*draws water from well, gives some to* JESUS. *He drinks.*)
Sir, you are drinking the very best of water.
The well is ancient, and is never dry.

JESUS
There is a well so deep it has no bottom.
There are truly living waters, not like these.
They spring from the great source no eye has seen.
The body does not know that it craves them.
The spirit knows, but cannot always find them.
This water that I drink is good, is good,
But I shall thirst again as time goes by.
Once you drink the waters of the soul,
Which I can give you, as you gave me this,
Your longings will be satisfied for ever.

WOMAN S. (*curious and intrigued, in spite of herself*)
How can this be? Are you some magician?
How do you know what longings I might have?

JESUS
Longings you cannot even define,
Dissatisfaction with the scheme of things,
Dissatisfaction with yourself, your life,
Your husband –

WOMAN S.
                    I do not have a husband.

JESUS (*looking at her*)
The man you live with is something else,
Is that it? Not the first, or second, either,
Am I right?

WOMAN S.
                    You cannot know these things,
    You are guessing.

JESUS
                        But I guessed correctly.
    Your life is laid out before me like a map.

WOMAN S.
    Well, we have shamans in Samaria.
    They wander up and down our holy mountain,
    Mount Gerizim, our place of the ancestors,
    They sing to the winds, they prophesy.
    You Jews think Jerusalem is all in all.

JESUS
    No place is sacred. Gerizim, Jerusalem,
    These could go in the twinkling of an eye.
    God makes sacred what he wants to make sacred,
    The desert, the sea-bed, the back of a star.
    Split a piece of wood: he is there.
    Lift up a stone: you will find him.

WOMAN S.
    You are very familiar with God's name.

JESUS
    Am I? Shall we talk about the weather?
    Life is too short, the age is too late
    To talk about the weather.

WOMAN S.
                        Who are you?

JESUS
    You have heard of Jesus the Nazarene,
    Even in Samaria?

WOMAN S.
                    'Even in Samaria'!

I suspect Samaritans will be around
Long after you and I are gone. But yes,
I know you, you preach, you attract crowds.
So why are you not getting on with your mission?
Why are you chatting with an unmarried wife?

JESUS
Rain falls on the married and the unmarried.
A woman at a well is more than armies
If the seed grows that's watered by my words.

WOMAN S.
You are a strange man, even a strange Jew.

JESUS
That's good. What I have to do is new.

(*Enter* PETER *and* JOHN *and other disciples, including* JUDAS,
with provisions they have bought in the city.)

JUDAS
By God, those prices were extortionate!

PETER
Judas, what did you expect? Samaritans
Don't mix and mell with Jews. They fleece them
Whenever they can. They are a lost tribe
As far as I am concerned.

JESUS
                  Peter,
This woman – a woman of spirit, I may say –
Is one of your Samaritans. We've talked
And will talk more. I want to see her city,
Her people. I shall talk to them all.

PETER
Ma'am, no disrespect. Our Jesus
Is ahead of us. Prejudices cling.

Words are blunt and impatient.
Our enmities grow such solemn beards
We are afraid to cut them, but we should.

WOMAN S. (*not entirely melted, but willing to call a truce*)
Gentlemen, I am sure we all have much to learn.

(JESUS *and the* WOMAN OF SAMARIA *move off,* JESUS *helping
her to carry the heavy water-jar.*)

JUDAS
What's he up to? Why give a cause of scandal
On a plate, if anyone was watching?
A woman on her own? Sitting talking to her
In the open air? A Samaritan at that!
He could hardly present a worse image!

JOHN
Oh I don't know. He is here to break conventions.
Is talking to a woman so terrible?
What think you, Peter?

PETER
                              It depends who saw them.
There are always figures lurking about an oasis.
Jews just don't hobnob with Samaritans,
Especially Samaritan women. Don't forget
Everything in our ambience is political.
We have enemies waiting to pounce.

JOHN
Jesus will not be hamstrung by prudence.

PETER
We have seen him being prudent, melting away
From impetuous crowds.

JOHN
                              He is beyond that now.

If he wants to bring Jew and Samaritan together,
If he wants to talk to women in the fields,
He takes the consequences.

JUDAS

                       She was a feisty one,
She will blab!

JOHN

                Let her blab the good tidings.
In the meantime let us sit and eat.

Act One Scene Three

A Jewish council chamber. Enter JETHRO, EZRA, REUBEN,
and a few priests and officials.

JETHRO

What exactly has this scummy Kohath been telling us, Reuben?

REUBEN

The Nazarene was seen talking intimately with a woman in the
open air.

JETHRO

An impropriety is hardly a capital offence.

REUBEN

This was in Samaria, at the old Jacob's well.

JETHRO

Samaria? What on earth was he doing there?

REUBEN

Said he was just passing through.

EZRA

But he stopped: why? Samaritans are not counted among our friends. He is as devious as they come.

JETHRO

He is mad. He is giving us another lever to move against him. What sort of Jew is he for God's sake?

Enter KOHATH

KOHATH

I have one more piece of news, gentlemen.

JETHRO

For which you will want one more piece of silver.

KOHATH

If it please you. The labourer is worthy of his hire.

JETHRO

Save us your proverbs, just give us the news.

KOHATH

I have it on good authority that Jesus will address a large gathering near Jerusalem later this week. The impression is that it might be important. I shall be there myself, but you may also want to plant some observers. Some say it could be his last chance to make his mission clear and dear to the people, which it certainly is not at the moment. Sceptics foretell a flight of rhetoric dropping a planeload of fudge. Either way, there's your man, your suspect, in full exposure. You may even find the woman of Samaria hanging on his words – or his arm.

EZRA

Kohath, there is no need for vulgarity. These are serious matters involving the security of the country.

KOHATH (*bows ironically*)

You are the masters. I take back anything you do not like.

JETHRO (*handing over money*)
   Leave us. We shall see what we shall see.

   (*Exit* KOHATH. *Buzz of discussion in council.*)

Act One Scene Four

*A hill outside Jerusalem. A crowd, shifting and whispering
expectantly. Enter* JESUS *with some of his disciples, including*
PETER, JOHN, *and* JUDAS.

JESUS
   Listen well. I have a story to tell.
   It may be I shall not have many chances
   To speak to you again. On a fine day
   You know how sometimes on the horizon
   A grey cloud rises, grows and spreads until
   Darkness is almost overhead. Almost.
   In the meantime, however, I have light.

   People complain I speak in parables.
   Even my disciples (*glances at them*) sometimes complain –
   Oh yes they do! But I am not a priest
   To rattle off the voices of his fathers
   As if there could be nothing new on earth.
   The new is here; I have it, show it, give it!
   Those who have ears to hear can always hear it.
   Reach out; think; listen; argue with me;
   Take a crossbow to the bloated belly of convention.
   I have not come to fulfil the prophets,
   Though some will say I have. I am myself
   A prophet never dreamed of; my remit
   (If I fulfil my life) is to free worlds,
   Not this one only, from guilt, hate, death itself.

You have all heard of the kingdom of heaven,
But it is not what you think it is.

1 VOICE
A republic!

2 VOICE
                    A commonwealth!

3 VOICE
                                        A bloody empire!

JESUS
We'll see, we'll see. But we must walk round it.
Take a mustard seed. Very small, is it not?
You wonder what could possibly come of it.
Goodness, it could sit in a sparrow's eye!
But plant it, water it, watch and wait for it.
It spreads, it bustles up like a bush, it's a tree, with branches,
Branches with birds, birds bursting into song.

A VOICE
What about the mustard?

JESUS
                    You get the mustard,
You get the mustard all right, for your meat,
But that is not the point of the parable.
What is the point of the parable?

A VOICE
Dinny despise the wee things.

JESUS
                            That's right.
Never despise children. Never despise the poor.
Never despise the outcast. But there's more.
The seed, the bush, the tree: it's a process.
The kingdom of heaven is not a thing,

Nor is it a place, it is alive, it grows.
Not even a Greek painter (and they are good)
Could set it before you.

A VOICE
                    Fuck the Greeks!

JESUS (*laughs*)
OK, but I will not be sidetracked.
I say again, it is not some Holy Grail
Cast in silver and kept in a cupboard.
Like everything in the universe, it lives.
It is not even something you can search for,
Though the paradox is that you must do so
With your heart and soul. Do you understand?

VOICES
No! – Not really! – Not a bit! – What is it?

JESUS
The kingdom of heaven is among you.
It is this very moment waving like leaves
And sending the most delicate roots in the world
Out through your doubts and the fears of the time.

A VOICE
You sound like mystical John, the poet!

ANOTHER VOICE
Tell us what you want us all to do!

JESUS (*speaks strongly, clearly, with authority*)
Sell what you have and give to the poor.
Love your enemies, not just your friends.
Forgive a brother or sister who offends you
Not seven but seventy-seven times.
Feed the starving and clothe the naked.
Welcome the refugee and the stranger.
Visit the hospital, visit the jail

Where your brothers and sisters suffer and groan.
And above all, a new commandment
From me, the new man and the son of man:
Love one another, as I have loved you.
Be loving, not judgemental, and be free.

(*Some parents in the crowd send out their children to meet Jesus.
The disciples step forward protectively but officiously to stop the
children coming near.*)

JESUS (*angry*)
Dear God, will you never learn? My disciples too!
Have you forgotten, or could you not believe me,
When I said, Let children talk to me,
Even little children, for they get vibrations
Of the kingdom of heaven that seem to pass
Right through your pursed lips and stiffened hides?
– Come, children, come over here beside me.

JUDAS (*mutters*)
Who is being judgemental now?

(*The disciples are somewhat shamefaced and bemused. They stand
back while Jesus walks a little way off and hunkers down. The
children run to him. We cannot hear what he says, but he makes
gestures with his arms and seems to be telling them a story. They
listen intently. The crowd disperses except for the parents of the
children. The disciples move further back, waiting for Jesus to
finish. Spotlight on Jesus and children.*)

Act One Scene Five

A nondescript room in KOHATH's *house. Enter* KOHATH.

KOHATH (*looking through the shorthand notes he has made of the meeting in Scene Four*)
    Surely he cannot survive after this.
    Surely he must know every word is recorded.
    Those eyes of his probably picked me out,
    Saw me scribbling, but did he pause,
    Did he fudge, did he accommodate,
    Did he hell! The man is either naive
    Beyond measure, which is hard to believe,
    Or is arrogant beyond measure, which I think
    Is possible, but only in a special sense,
    An extraordinary sense that withdraws the sting.
    I have never heard such authority.
    Where does it come from? Not from Nazareth!
    Something is going to happen: I can feel it.
    Well, I am glad to say it's no problem of mine!
    I am no councillor, I am no commandant.
    I am only poor Kohath who takes notes
    And turns them into money. Rich pickings
    When revolutionaries spill the beans in public,
    And if Jesus is not a revolutionary
    I'll throw my tablets into Galilee!
    But who is for the historical chop?
    Who is the enemy? The Romans? The Jews?
    This is where slivers, delicious slivers
    Of ambiguity, profitable slivers
    Are thrust slithering into the system.
    Oh my head's in the clouds when I think of it,
    I'm up on stilts to scan the horizon
    For the first hint of grapeshot from the Forum,
    For the first ram's-horn tocsin from the Temple!
    And do you know I have such long fingers
    I can dip them in the bottom of the glue-pot
    Before I guddle for the shining ones

And grasp, and grin, and gasp, and gather up
The wages, some might say of sin, but really
Of my most nimble Machiavellianism.
Pharisees first, I think; centurions next;
Then I must not forget my dear Judas
Who is ripe for dissection and disaffection.
Come all ye high cats and be cool.
Come to Kohath's school.
You pay, I rule.

Act Two Scene One

A Roman command post. The COMMANDANT *is talking to two of his* CENTURIONS.

COMMANDANT
So what did Kohath say about the Jews?

1 CENTURION
He says they are in a dangerous mood. He says we ought to be pre-
pared for anything from now on. It will soon be the time of their
Passover, when Jerusalem will be packed thick with pilgrims.

COMMANDANT
Zealots?

1 CENTURION
Some, certainly. But it is a holiday occasion. People come from all
over, even from abroad.

COMMANDANT
A spark could ignite demonstrations, or worse?

2 CENTURION
Our informer thinks so. That's his warning. He has usually not
been far wrong in the past.

COMMANDANT
But the people in general? Has this man Jesus been stirring them
up?

1 CENTURION
Yes and no. We are still not sure, and it is maddening. I would say
no rather than yes, but the crowds he collects are now very great
and who knows what crowd psychology can make of moral uplift?

COMMANDANT
Did Kohath give details of the man's harangues?

2 CENTURION

Yes, he had full notes, for which he was well paid.

COMMANDANT

Trust no one in the Middle East, my father used to say. Well, we are stuck with this scarecrow. Was the sermon, if that's what you call it, subversive?

1 CENTURION

It was more like a seminar than a sermon, sir. He invited questions, and got them. That's why he's so hard to pin down. He's no Savonarola.

COMMANDANT

Specifically, what was subversive, potentially subversive?

1 CENTURION

The Jews are to sell their goods and help the poor.

COMMANDANT

How can the poor help the poor? The crowds he addresses are not exactly millionaires. Are we going to have a new generation of people sleeping rough and banging their begging-bowls on our pavements?

1 CENTURION

I only report what Kohath says he said.

COMMANDANT

It looks to me as if he *does* want to disrupt society. Why on earth are reformers so keen on poverty?

2 CENTURION

That's not what he says, sir. It's more equality than poverty.

COMMANDANT

Bankrolling poverty doesn't remove it. It's a canker in the system. Needs politics, not emotion.

1 CENTURION
  Well, perhaps he *is* political.

COMMANDANT
  How come?

2 CENTURION
  If he encouraged the Jews to revolt against the huge disparities of wealth in the Roman Empire –

COMMANDANT
  Never. It won't happen. If the Jews had power they would be just as mercantile as we are. D'you think they'd pass up caviar and Chianti Classico just because they saw a beggar in the gutter?

2 CENTURION
  Jesus says they *ought* to. He's a visionary. He's a missionary. People listen. His disciple John says much about language, about the power of words.

COMMANDANT
  Well, you have still to convince me. But I reckon it is a point, and we have to take it on board. I have read enough history to know that demagogues are dangerous. Palestine at Passover will be a tinderbox. Multiply guards on all our public buildings. Arrest Jews who congregate too obviously in public places. But keep the mailed fist at arm's length, if you know what I mean. Riots in Jerusalem are not what we want, though if Kohath is right it may come to that. Does it strike you that perhaps that is what he wants? He is as devious as a corkscrew, that one. Watch him. Watch everybody! (*laughs*)

1 CENTURION
  I know, sir. It's that sort of time.

2 CENTURION
  And Jesus is the eye of the cyclone – if there is a cyclone.

Act Two Scene Two

KOHATH'*s room. It is rather bleak, but is filled with carefully*
arranged packages of documents – the files of a master spy.
Enter KOHATH, SIMON, *and* JUDAS.

KOHATH

Well, gentlemen, have you come to any conclusions about the
future of the itinerant preacher?

SIMON

You tell us there is no chance of an uprising?

KOHATH

None whatsoever. The whole liberation movement is stagnant.
Since Jude was killed by the Romans, the Zealots according to my
enquiries are as good as leaderless. Nahum, Jude's successor, may
be very sincere, but he lacks the drive and forward planning of a
real leader, and his followers are confused and discontented.
Whatever the future may hold, the charisma of Zealotry at the
moment has been poured away.

SIMON

Is this the truth?

KOHATH

Would I tell a lie?

SIMON

If it is true, it is the end of a great dream. When I see all those
Roman statues, Roman arms, Roman proclamations, when I hear
the cursed tramp of a legion through the street, when I listen to that
upstart language – *hic haec hoc* – lording it over the ancient music
of Hebrew and Aramaic, I want to hide, I want to howl, I want to
hit something that is not there. How did we come to this? Judas,
your hopes were my hopes. What did we do or not do to bring us
to that dried-up river-bed?

JUDAS

That's an easy one. We traced the wrong river. We followed the wrong leader. Jesus was never going to arm us. Or even to organize us. He is besotted with godliness. If Palestine goes down the tubes, he will give an eloquent sigh and go fishing. Our people were searching for a Messiah who would slice off the Roman yoke like a militant angel and give them back a transformed land where all things would be made new. Well, we haven't got that Messiah. Perhaps we thought we had.

SIMON

There's no perhaps! We did think so, and act so. That is what is so bad.

KOHATH

Gentlemen, if I may interrupt. As I'm sure you know, I am a practical sort of fellow, and I hate to observe devoted and intelligent men bumbazed by a bolt from the blue. Jesus is not your man. Can I sow a little seed – say a mustard seed – of retaliation – let us not call it vengeance – for your wrecked hopes and political disarray. I have told you that there is no rebellion on the cards. In that case, will you not direct your energies – your disappointed energies – against the perpetrator of that disappointment?

JUDAS

Do I smell what you mean?

KOHATH

I think you do.

SIMON

But how?

KOHATH

You cannot do it by yourselves. But I have a sort of grand plan, still inchoate, which will involve both Jews and Romans in a species of Götterdämmerung. Your man will not survive, I assure you.

JUDAS

Once the plot has been plotted, tell me. Simon will support me, but I am upfront in this.

SIMON

Surely.

JUDAS

He has betrayed the liberation of our country. I shall betray him in turn.

KOHATH

There will be money in it.

JUDAS

Better still.

KOHATH

We shall speak again about this. In the meantime, silence.

JUDAS

Of course.

SIMON

Of course.

Act Two Scene Three

A simple room in a house used by JESUS. *He is sitting at a table, reading a document. Enter* MARY MAGDALENE, *agitated. He rises.*

JESUS

Mary Magdalene! What is wrong? What has happened?

MARY M.

I would like to know what has happened!

I have never seen so many armed soldiers
Prowling and scowling along the streets.
I was asked many times for my I.D.,
And that is not unusual, but this time
They scanned it closely like state interrogators,
Dismissing me with 'Watch where you go!'
I am fairly certain I was not followed,
Came here deviously. I am streetwise
As you know. But I had to warn you.
There is an air of – it's hard to describe,
Like a storm struggling through the time barrier
To break on us –

JESUS

　　　　　　　Thank God you are safe,
But you are not safe here. *I* am not safe here.
Palestine swarms with spies, hired, freelance,
Disguised like beggars, water-sellers, tax-collectors,
Priests even. Nothing cannot be cloned.
I do not stay long in one place now.
Do the Romans know something we don't know?
Why this sudden vigilance and padding about?

MARY M.

Some say your last speech was too radical.

JESUS

Forgive your brother, love your neighbour. Radical?

MARY M.

Love your *enemy*, you said. That gets them worried.
They think it might be in code, for an uprising.

JESUS

And so it might, but not as they understand it.
You were in the crowd. How did they react?

MARY M.

Some were inspired; some grumbled it was too hard.
Whichever way, the interest was intense.

JESUS

Were there note-takers?

MARY M.

Oh yes, several.

JESUS

It is brewing; it is coming; I can feel it.

MARY M.

I have brought you bad tidings. Forgive me.

JESUS

My dear, you cannot bring me anything but good.
Whatever happens, you are one of those
I have bound to my heart. Of followers
You are the first. The world will know it.
You will not desert me if bad things come,
When bad things come, as I think they will.
You have been through much, you are strong.

MARY M.

If I am strong, Jesus, you made me so.
When I lay in that pit of self-distrust
So long ago, oh not so long ago,
When I thought my life was unravelling
Steadily into shreds and fragments of sense,
You lifted me, you made me whole again.

JESUS

It may be you will need all your strength.
It may be I too will need all mine.
Foreboding feels about with icy claw
Into the channels of my blood. Not yet,
O God! I have so many things to do –

(*A shout outside. A hammering on the door.* JESUS *and* MARY M.
*freeze, staring at each other. And then – thank God! – only the
voice of a drunk as he passes singing along the street:*)

DRUNK MAN

>The taxman counts his silver
>The soldier counts his scars
>The jailer counts his prisoners
>As his baton bangs the bars
>
>O drink up to the living
>Because they are not dead
>The time will come when cinders
>Are gnashed instead of bread
>
>Are gnashed are gnashed they tell us
>At a table with the shades
>We'd rather sure be dancing
>In gardens and in glades
>
>So give me the old flagon
>We'll fill him to the brim
>We'll pat him on the belly
>And then we'll empty him

MARY M. (*smiles*)

>Is that the bad spell broken? Life goes on.
>How many apprehensive souls are waiting
>For that knock on the door which may not come –

JESUS (*smiles too, but is still troubled*)

>True, true. But I must regard myself
>As a marked man. I shall press forward,
>Watching my back. I may disguise myself.
>You may not see me for a while,
>But I cannot be a fugitive from your soul.
>That song is in my head. Bread and wine –
>Yes, both are good. Why do people stare
>Or shake their heads or shuffle off
>When I tell them I am the true vine,
>When I tell them I am the bread of life?
>Even my disciples frown and look shifty.

MARY M. (*bantering*)
   I know why, but I shall not tell you.

JESUS
   Oh women, women, I know you know everything!

MARY M.
   You must not ask rhetorical questions.

JESUS
   Touché. I am not myself. The fears
   That crowd on me are new and terrible.
   I have to deal with them, and shall do.
   I fear for your life too, my dear. Take care,
   You must not be seen with me. Go first.
   I shall cloak myself and melt off later.
   It sounds like thunder. The air is stifling.
   Well, it is God's air, and what we can
   We must do.

MARY M.
                    Jesus, take every care.
   Pass any message by the usual source.   (*they embrace briefly*)

(*A loud crack of thunder.* MARY M. *covers her head and hurries
out.* JESUS *is left, looking at the door as if to call her back, in a
flash of lightning.*)

Act Two Scene Four

*A dark evening. Intermittent thunder and lightning. A street. Enter
a* MAD PROPHET, *strangely dressed, muttering, sometimes singing,
sometimes denouncing. He tries to buttonhole passers-by, who
hurry past him on their way home before the storm breaks.*

MAD PROPHET
   Good folk! Bad folk! Listen, listen. It's not growing dark for

nothing, you know. Buzz, buzz, buzz. Can you hear it? Beelzebub is up. The lord of the flies is awake. The air will be swarming with demons. Is your sin on your back? Are your sins in a pack? Is it a six-pack or a six-hundred-pack? Oh sir, you sir, you know there's no going back. There's going black (*laughs wildly*) but not back. Flames for sinners, flames and cinders. Wouldn't you be glad to eat grass, like Nebuchadnezzar? You'll eat dust and be thankful. A chiel's amang ye, no takin notes, he's takin *you*!

(*sings*)   O Cain slew Abel
                With the leg of a table
                And got a mark on his brow.
                When you see him coming
                Start the drumming
                It won't be too long now.

No, ma'am, it can't be long. Have you bought your shroud? Have you sharpened your trowel? Show me your hand. No? It doesn't matter, I can see through flesh and stuff, I can see your life-line. Gey faint, lady, gey faint. (*laughs*) (*she snatches herself away*) Here's a fine young man. Are you going to a party? Are you going to dance among the dead ones? All the dead bald grinning bony girls, eh? Hurry away. Seize the day. Lift your flute and play.

            By cool Siloam's shady rill
            It's too late now to take a pill. (*he shrieks with laughter*)

Are you all going to leave me alone? I was going to give you a sermon, just a little sermon. It's gone out of my head for the moment, but I know it was tremendous, absolutely tremendous. It would galvanize the gates of Gath, it would astound the ashpits of Ashkelon. (*crack of thunder*) (*the* PROPHET *shakes his fist*) Yes, yes, old thunderer, old father, old flamethrower, old furtive one that no one ever sees, I'll get you yet, I'll catch you in a net, I'll not let you forget. (*the* PROPHET *stumbles off, muttering.*)

Act Three Scene One

A Jewish council chamber. Enter the High Priest CAIAPHAS,
JETHRO, EZRA, REUBEN, *and various priests and officials.*
A bell sounds, to mark the opening of an important session.

CAIAPHAS

Gentlemen, we have only one item on the agenda, but I guess you
will agree with me that it is important, since it affects both the faith
and the state. The first is ours, the second is not. But we are so intimately bound up with the state by so many laws and obligations,
as well as by the brute realities of foreign rule, that our actions
must stride across politics as well as ethics. We are here to discuss
the case of the Nazarene preacher, Jesus. I begin by reminding you
that Jesus is a Jew, and comes from a respectable Jewish family.
He is not some wild hairy desert hermit who has seen God in a
sandstorm and rushes to bowl the world over with his hot revela-
tion. Jesus is educated, speaks well and clearly. He is not bristling
with either knives or lice. I take him seriously, on his own terms.
But –

JETHRO

High time you came to the 'but', if I may say so.

CAIAPHAS

This is not a kangaroo court. My duty is to lay everything before
you. It may be that a man's life is at stake. Our concern has to
centre on the fact that the normal pre-Passover excitement which
has been building up in Palestine is shot through with elements of
unease and foreboding. Where do the unease and foreboding come
from? Rightly or wrongly, people in high places point the finger at
Jesus –

JETHRO

Rightly!

REUBEN

Wrongly, till proved.

CAIAPHAS
- who has been called agitator, anarchist, zealot, blasphemer, heretic, sabbath-breaker, beggar-lover, prostitute-fancier, temple-defier, and as many other names as prejudice could think up. As he is not armed, and has not, so far as we know, stockpiled arms for his disciples and followers, it is hard to see why he has become such a bogyman to some.

JETHRO
Power of the word, gift of the gab.

EZRA
Born dissenter.

REUBEN
Curiosity factor - he remains enigmatic.

CAIAPHAS
Yet he is a Jew, and he says he is a prophet. We have had many prophets in the past, and some have been difficult characters, to put it mildly.

JETHRO
I don't think I want a prophet who hires thugs to drive lawful merchants out of the temple. You say he has not armed his followers, and that may be true, but he was quite happy to bring a posse of hardmen to scare the moneylenders out of their wits. It seems that he is given to violent outbursts of this kind. The fact that I am a Pharisee can hardly stop me from deploring the extraordinary and much-talked-about verbal onslaught (thank God it *was* only verbal this time!) which he made against all Pharisees and Scribes (yes, you too, Scribe Reuben!). What did he call us? - brood of vipers, blind guides, hypocrites, children of hell. He was wound up, he was raging. He talks of love, but there's a depth of violence in him that makes him dangerous, or if you want me to be very correct, a potential danger. And therefore I think we must do something about him.

CAIAPHAS
Reuben?

REUBEN

I agree that he sometimes goes over the top. But a case could be made for saying that this comes from the strength of his feeling about things that are wrong: sometimes the only way to initiate change is to exaggerate, to hammer home, to shame people. We Scribes and Pharisees are not much given to self-examination. Perhaps we should be.

CAIAPHAS

And Ezra?

EZRA

A Sadducee could never feel kindly towards someone who makes light of ancient institutions and puts beggars and prostitutes and tax-collectors ahead of those who sit in solemn council.

CAIAPHAS

I go back to what Jethro said about Jesus being a potential danger. What is this danger? I began by defending him, but there are questions that will not go away. No one so far has mentioned the word Rome. Everything we discuss here is provisional, since we do not have the power of a Jewish national assembly. And it is not only Zealots who would like to see a Jewish national assembly. The idea is quite widespread among the populace. If Jesus continues to preach and to prosper, and to attract followers, the Jewish dimension of a national prophet will begin to alarm the Romans, and the slightest hint of a mass movement could result in fearful oppression and reprisals. We have painfully reached, over the years, a working accommodation with Rome –

REUBEN

– which some say is cowardly and unworthy –

CAIAPHAS

– which some say is cowardly and unworthy, but which sensible citizens accept as necessary –

REUBEN

– until the real uprising takes place –

CAIAPHAS
> – if it ever does, and I don't deny that possible scenario. But in the
> meantime we live under the shadow of the power of Rome. The
> soldiers are in the streets, and their hands are on their swords. Even
> Reuben will agree that at this precise moment in time we cannot
> allow an agitator – charismatic as they say he is – to risk toppling
> the fragile but ancient mass of Jewish Palestine into the abyss.

JETHRO
> Which means – ?

CAIAPHAS
> That our plan must be to stop his mouth. He must be killed.

REUBEN
> This is a big step.

EZRA
> No no, let us do it.

CAIAPHAS
> It is a big step, but I would rather one man should die than a nation
> be destroyed.

Act Three Scene Two

Outside a council office. JUDAS *stands uncertainly at the entrance,*
waiting to go in to betray Jesus. Now that the actual moment has
come, he is less brash about what he still intends to do.

JUDAS
> Are they trying to make it easy for me?
> Look how the high priest has put up a notice
> Saying that Jesus is now on the run
> And may even be disguised, but anyone

Knowing his whereabouts – *I* do, *I* do! –
Should report it to the authorities
Who have signed a warrant for his arrest.
Arrest! So I cannot assassinate him,
It is taken out of my hands. I pass the guilt
On this unexpected plate to the priests.
They will know what to do with him!
Oh yes, there's no love lost with the temple!
But why should I worry about guilt?
I am doing what has to be done.
Jesus King of Palestine, what a joke.
Jesus President of the Republic –
Side-splitting. Jesus Slave of God,
That's more like it, and we don't need slaves.
I wash my hands of our association
Which once – it seems so long ago –
I wanted to prosper. He had a hook
That went right into my soul
In those days, into my soul.
I would have said it was for ever.
But there is no going back. It is finished.
I can almost see his eyes looking at me
But it is finished. Leave me, Jesus!
I cannot stand any more of you,
I cannot stand your heaven, do you hear me?
Hills and waters of beloved Palestine
Are all I want, its fruits, its lakes, its skies.
I hate you that you killed it down the wind,
Your land, my land, our poor oppressed land.
Go to heaven or hell. You failed me is all.

(*he knocks at the gate, to enter the office*)

Act Three Scene Three

Inside the council office. JUDAS *is given an audience with* JETHRO.

JETHRO
You have some information? What is your name?

JUDAS
My name is Judas, and I am one of the Nazarene's disciples. I follow him as he goes about the country.

JETHRO
But we are told that he has gone to ground. He must have learned that he is in danger.

JUDAS
True. But it will not be hard for me to track him down.

JETHRO
He is a Jew. You are a Jew. Why should you want to betray him?

JUDAS
He is a fallen idol. I thought he would lead us into the Promised Land.

JETHRO
You are in the Promised Land. Palestine is the home of the Jews, who are God's chosen people.

JUDAS (*laughs bitterly*)
God has a strange conception of a home! We are tenants, not owners. Our landlord is a man of iron, an emperor with a gun at his hip, barking his orders out like bronze inscriptions!

JETHRO
I remind you that we have a concordat with that emperor. The balance between Rome and Jerusalem is delicate, difficult, but damn necessary.

JUDAS

You say. Some do not say. I do not say. I want a change. The Nazarene cannot deliver that change, which gives me a personal reason for hating him.

JETHRO

I am always a little suspicious of renegades. Turn once, you may turn again.

JUDAS

Never! I have had it up to here with Jesus!

JETHRO

Very well, we shall take you on board. You will not make any effort yourself to capture or injure the man. That is for the council, and eventually for the Roman authorities, to deal with. What we require of you is simply to find and point out the preacher, who may be disguised (or so we are told), in order that we and our Roman allies can move in and make the arrest.

JUDAS

Allies? Aliens!

JETHRO

All right, all right. You are sure you have no other motive?

JUDAS

I was told there would be a reward.

JETHRO

I thought so. You disgust me. You make a great show of idealism and public service – let us cleanse the land of foreign oppressors – but underneath it all you are a man of greed, straining your ears for the jingle of shekels –

JUDAS

It isn't shekels – would that it was! The bloody coins are Roman!

JETHRO

I've had enough of you (*goes to a large box, unlocks it, turns to* JUDAS). Twenty pieces of silver.

JUDAS
Forty.

JETHRO
Thirty, and that's final (*puts the silver into a bag and hands it over*). Remember your promise to us. Identify Jesus. After that you may do what you will. Unlike some, I am not a prophet, but that bag of silver – it's quite heavy, you know – may become a millstone hanging round your neck.

JUDAS
I doubt it. I know what to do with money. Spending it warms the soul.

JETHRO
You have no soul. Now clear out. I am busy.

JUDAS
Oh hoity-toity. A Pharisee to the end. Thanks for the silver.

(*Exit* JUDAS. JETHRO *stares after him, frowns, shakes his head*)

Act Three Scene Four

The Last Supper. Evening. Lamps are lit. An upper room with low ceiling, giving the impression of intimacy and secrecy. JESUS *and the* TWELVE DISCIPLES *are reclining at a long low table which has been set for a simple meal,* JOHN *the beloved disciple reclining close to him on his left, and* PETER, *sitting more upright, on his right.* JUDAS *is at one end,* SIMON *at the other.*

JESUS
Many suppers, many Passovers. It is good when people can be gathered together. Yet I think this is the last time when we shall all be together (*cries and gestures of disbelief*). Yes, it is the last time,

and you must prepare yourselves for a scattering, for suffering, for good and bad things, triumphs and persecutions, when I am no longer with you.

PETER

How should you not be with us? Are you going on a journey?

JESUS

I am going where you cannot follow me.

PETER

Is there any such place? You are like a hero, a trailblazer, a Moses, a Germanic prince. Your followers would die for you.

JESUS

Words are easy, Peter. God may hold you to your promise.

ANDREW

But what has happened to cause this change? Is there some disaster looming, and we don't know about it?

JESUS

There is, and there is not.

SIMON

Oh, riddles again!

JESUS

Bear with me. What began as forebodings is now standing on the very cusp of fact. I knew that I was being watched, my words being recorded. I knew that my actions had caused disquiet. My cleansing of the temple made me enemies. My downgrading of the Sabbath and of ritual observances in general made me more. Even my gift of healing raised suspicion. If I spoke to a woman on her own, in the open air, I was a monster. When I championed the poor and castigated the rich, I was an anarchist. But above all, when I talked about the kingdom of heaven, I threatened the cosy Rome-Jerusalem axis and sent it teetering and tottering into history. In short, I became history. I want a new order of things. Jerusalem and Rome cannot stand this, and are going to get rid of me.

(*cries and gasps of anger around the table*)

Oh yes, they are manoeuvring my removal by a betrayal at this very moment.

(*He passes a written note down the table to* JUDAS, *who goes white, stands up abruptly, and leaves the room. The other disciples are surprised, but not alarmed, as they do not know about* JUDAS*'s plot.*)

SIMON
And why is this not a disaster?

JESUS
Think of that old mustard-seed of mine. If the seed had not been covered with the darkness of the earth, and become dead to the eye, there would be neither bush nor branch, nor anything green, anything full of savour, anything full of goodness, to spread through the light of the fields. If I die, I shall be with you to the end of the world. What is heaven? What is earth? Both – yes, even heaven – may pass away, but my words will not pass away. That is my kingdom. And Caesar and Herod are kings in a sort of dumb-show. The play drives past them. They do not like that, they kick out. But they shall kick me into my second life.

JOHN
Comfort us a little.

JESUS (*takes bread, breaks it into little pieces, and passes it round the table*)
Bread is a living thing, like flesh. Eat this, which I give you from my own hands, and think you are absorbing the life I am about to lose.

(*takes a large goblet of wine and passes it round the table*)

Wine is a living thing, like blood. Drink this, which I give you from my own hands, and think you are absorbing the life I am about to lose.

(The disciples eat and drink, in silence, but it remains informal, not ritualistic. After a while JESUS *stands and makes a gesture with his arms as if to cover everything with a blessing, but does not speak. He leaves the room.)*

PETER

If this is our last supper, let us go in peace. And let us be strong for any storm that is about to break.

Act Three Scene Five

A street. JUDAS *is leaning against a wall, muttering to himself. Enter* SIMON, *angry.*

SIMON

Judas, I have just learned about your visit to Jethro.

JUDAS

Oh yes?

SIMON

We were going to do this thing together, remember?

JUDAS

Oh well, I got to thinking about it. It wasn't really a job for two, Simon.

SIMON

You swore, before Kohath, that we had a pact between us to bring Jesus down.

JUDAS

Well, I broke the pact, didn't I?

SIMON

And I suppose you are getting paid for it.

JUDAS

Of course. I made the running. You always seemed a bit luke-warm. I decided to act. To him who hath shall be given. Now go away. I have things to think about.

SIMON

You bastard! I bet it was the money that tipped the scale. You would do a thing like that for a few pieces of silver.

JUDAS

Thirty, to be precise.

SIMON

Half of that should have been mine.

JUDAS

Well, it won't be now. In any case

(suddenly realizing he has a defence)

don't blame me. Blame Kohath. It was Kohath who brought us together on this. Without him, nothing would have happened. We'd be simmering away with discontent and leaving everything to fate. He's the one who unlocked the gears and got things going.

SIMON

I'll kill Kohath.

JUDAS

I doubt it. You have to be up *very* early in the morning to put salt on that one's tail. Anyhow, as I said, I've many things to do, so just fuck off, will you. You're a second-rater, Simon.

SIMON

And you don't rate at all. You're off the scale, Judas. There's nothing more to say.

(exeunt in different directions)

Act Four Scene One

The Garden of Gethsemane. Night. Enter JESUS *and several disciples, including* PETER, JOHN, *and* JAMES. *They are tired, and Gethsemane is a place they sometimes visit for rest and recuperation, a secluded spot on the lower slopes of the Mount of Olives near Jerusalem. They sit in the shade of the olive-trees.*

PETER

Safe from the mob, for a few hours at anyrate! These last days have been hectic. Pilgrims, donkeys, money-changers, chattering families, priests' servants with baskets of laundered robes, Romans barking orders, the usual Passover crowd but something more – a buzz, a whisper, suspicion, sidelong looks, a sudden silence and then it all breaks out again. What was that exotic proverb you heard, James?

JAMES

May you live in interesting times. But it's a curse rather than a proverb. It's Chinese. A conservative society *would* say that. I don't hold with it. I wouldn't live at any other time than ours, when who knows what will happen to either Rome or Jerusalem in the next hundred years. All that is solid melts into air.

PETER

It's interesting but it's tiring! Do we want shouts and shrieks, processions, batons, blood on the streets – stuff of life, inescapable, insufferable –

JAMES

– or so we say, but it's all sufferable – story of the omelette –

PETER

– crack a few heads or eggs – might be ours though –

JAMES (*yawns*)

If we are to be broken, we should get some sleep first. The night is warm, the ground is soft, the oil lies dreaming in the olive-trees.

JOHN

Brother James, it's no time for poetry. There is fear in the air.

JESUS

Let it be a waking sleep. We have enemies. The darkness is full of
eyes. Let a feather rouse you.

(The disciples, leaning against trees, fall into an uneasy sleep.
JESUS *walks some distance away, to think and pray by himself.)*

It is dark outside, and in my mind.
Who is there now except God?
I can put my case and treat with him,
Since we are free, I know that we are free.
What is my case, that we all want to live?
Death, in this grove, breathes on me like a wolf.
My skin creeps, my hair bristles, I shrink
From what I know must hurt me and must win.
Old age with all its ills would be a blessing,
But I am sure death cannot wait for me.
Well then, I cannot wait for death, I am ready.
It is hard, God knows, do you hear me?
I could wish it all to be undone,
The whole tapestry torn to shreds,
And start again without need of you,
God, God of death, God of sacrifice,
Why should I talk of you so kindly,
Holding my hand out for the poisoned cup?
Oh if you will take my real distress,
Clasp it, mark it, think of it still,
Then what you will, I will.

(The moon appears from behind a cloud, suddenly revealing
the figure of SATAN.)

SATAN

My old friend. We meet again. Darkness
Cannot hide you from me or me from you.
I find you in a great anxiety.
I shall not say I do not know the cause,

I do indeed, and I must sympathize.   (JESUS *looks at him grimly*)
Oh yes, it's true. When you spoke there to God
I thought you sketched out quite a decent case,
But you had something of a struggle, no?

(JESUS *is about to speak, but remains silent*)

I continue. You paddled your boat of doubts
So near the rapids of blasphemy (don't you like
These metaphors – oh poetry is everywhere!)
That I began throbbing with expectation.
You panted, you sweated, I saw it.
Now, I said to myself, now is the time
To resume our interrupted intercourse.

JESUS
I know your self-esteem keeps you trying,
But you will jangle all my nerves in vain.

SATAN
I wonder. Let me see, let me unfold.
I have to shake your unwise resolution.
A night scene is just right for this,
Shadowy shrubs and broken moonlight, owls
Hooting occasionally (or perhaps they are signals?),
Uncertain rustlings, a huddled mass
Of exhausted disciples – into this I come
With my most unwelcome thoughts. Jesus,
Listen well, as you say to the crowds.
You know there is a warrant for your arrest?

JESUS
I know.

SATAN
You could escape: Egypt, Syria?

JESUS
Unthinkable. What I do, I do here.

SATAN

   After arrest, what then? Is that thinkable?

JESUS

   It is in God's hands.

SATAN

                   On the contrary,
   It is in the hands of Caiaphas.
   The high priest does not want you to survive.
   He will hand you over to the Romans
   Who have ways of preventing survival.
   I suggest you are a reluctant martyr.
   Why not retire? A small farm, perhaps,
   Hens and a goat and good olive-trees,
   With your mother and Helen (is it?) and Anna,
   Where you could do God's work in an acre?

JESUS

   Satan, you are losing your grip.
   I have a mission. Crowds and cities
   Wait for me, dead or alive. God
   Is terrible. Death is terrible. But life
   Would be more terrible if I kept it,
   Feeding hens and leaning on a spade,
   Ochone, ochone, as the sun goes down.
   I understand I have to die, all right?

SATAN

   Tell me, have you seen a crucifixion?

          (JESUS *shakes his head*)

   Death may take many hours, or even days.
   When the nails are in, and you are hoisted up,
   I would be surprised if you did not cry out.
   Tens of thousands have done it before you.
   The strain, the pain, hanging in the sun
   Hour after hour, the thirst, the bloated tongue,
   The cramps and spasms (for you don't just loll there

Like a rag doll), and then the head drawn back
In a wild rictus as you gasp for air,
For slow asphyxiation, and release –
Oh, I should have been a painter,
Don't you think?

JESUS

                  The only art you know
Is to deceive, break down, induce despair –

SATAN

    – as I have almost done. You are pale,
Galilean, you are shaking, my dart
Is in your side. Are you so very sure
You want to change the course of history?
Topple my empire? End our conversations?

     (An owl hoots, and is answered. There are voices, rustlings,
                    snapping of twigs.)

JESUS

Satan, it is too late. You tried, and lost.
Go back to your own place, and count the cost.

       (SATAN vanishes. JESUS rouses his disciples.)

Peter, John, James, wake up, get up!
It is no time for sleep. History is here.
One age of time has come to an end,
Another age is throwing off its shell.

*(Enter JUDAS with a posse of soldiers. The soldiers are armed with
  swords and clubs. Behind them is quite a crowd of priests and
   temple police, many of them with lanterns and torches. It is a
rough, unruly, menacing scene. Because JESUS and his disciples are
cloaked against the night air, the soldiers are a little uncertain of
their prey. JUDAS steps forward, embraces and kisses JESUS. This
signal initiates the arrest, and JESUS is seized, bound, and marched
off without resistance. The disciples are not arrested, and disperse,
  shaken and dispirited, in the wake of the soldiers and police.)*

Act Four Scene Two

Day. A field with a grove of trees. Crows caw intermittently
throughout the scene. Enter JUDAS *slowly, almost as if*
sleepwalking, carrying a small bag. The bounce has gone out of
him since his last encounter with Simon.)

JUDAS
   What we thought we wanted, when we get it,
   Crumbles to dust. Too late to learn that,
   Too late to undo. Oh the adrenalin
   In Gethsemane, it was pumping,
   I was fired up through the darkness,
   Waiting till the disciples were asleep,
   Listening to Jesus muttering to himself.
   I stepped into the centre of the scene.
   Someone shone a lantern as I kissed him.
   No one could describe the look he gave me –
   Reproach, pity, even complicity,
   As if he knew what it was I had to do,
   Fulfilling something we were both a part of.
   All that is over, it's done, it's gone.
   He is as good as dead, and so am I.
   What is there to live for? Palestine?
   Bah, that will never happen. My heart
   Is emptied out, rattles like a gourd.
   I did not realize I needed you,
   Jesus. I have nothing to need now.

   (*He opens the bag and takes out a length of rope, climbs*
   the tree to fix it on a branch, makes a noose and hangs
   himself, inefficiently. As his body is struggling and gasping,
   enter KOHATH.)

KOHATH
   Friend Judas, you are doing the right thing.
   You did the deed I wanted, that was all.
   What more could life demand of you than this –

(KOHATH *seizes* JUDAS's *legs and pulls down sharply; the neck is broken, the body slumps.* KOHATH *lifts the bag* JUDAS *has left on the ground. Thirty pieces of silver jingle.* KOHATH *whistles, and pockets the silver.*)

Now there's a sweet reward for work well done.

(*Enter* SIMON, *who has been searching for* JUDAS. *He looks dangerous.*)

KOHATH (*cocky but nervous*)
Simon! Are you looking for a hanging?

SIMON
Kohath! Did you do this?

KOHATH
Certainly not. Why should I?

SIMON
Because no one ever knows what you are really up to.

KOHATH
I was passing along, and saw the body swaying in the breeze.

SIMON
Had Judas been paid?

KOHATH
I've no idea. There was nothing on the body.

SIMON
It was probably in the bag and you have snaffled it. Half of that money is mine – whole of it now that Judas is dead.

KOHATH (*draws dagger*)
You want to search me?

SIMON (*also draws a knife*)
I did not come unprepared.

(They fight, lunging at each other with the blades. KOHATH *yelps as a slash on his arm draws blood, but he is the nimbler of the two and stabs* SIMON *fatally in the chest.)*

KOHATH

Ten disciples now -- a nice round number. I shall at once inform the Romans. I've no doubt they'll rejoice at the demise of two Zealots, and pay me appropriately. A good morning's work. It's just a matter of being in the right place at the right time. I shall flourish like the green bay tree. (*He gives a little jig*) I leave the carrion to the crows.

ACT FOUR SCENE THREE

A council chamber, set up as a court. The first trial of Jesus. Enter the high priest CAIAPHAS, *who presides;* JETHRO, REUBEN, EZRA *and other priests and elders;* JESUS, *bound;* POLICEMEN; *and several* WITNESSES, *waiting to be called.*

CAIAPHAS

The defendant is permitted to make an opening statement.

JESUS

Why was I arrested like a common criminal, at dead of night, by armed men? Did you think I was going to knock a few heads together and make my escape? I have not promoted my teachings in secret. I have spoken in the fields, in synagogues and temples, freely and candidly, as many could testify. If you want to know what these teachings are, ask the public.

POLICEMAN (*striking* JESUS *on the face*)

Is that any way to answer the high priest?

JESUS

If I have said anything wrong, spell it out. If I have said what is right, why did you strike me?

CAIAPHAS

Never mind the niceties. You are hardly in a position to complain. If you will not defend yourself by giving us a résumé of what you and your disciples hope to achieve, I shall proceed with the witnesses we have gathered together.

JESUS

No doubt it will be a careful choice.

> (*The* POLICEMAN *is about to hit* JESUS *again, but* CAIAPHAS
> *signals to him not to do it.*)

CAIAPHAS

Call Witness No. 1.

> (WITNESS 1 *stands forward*)

What have you heard that is relevant to this enquiry?

WITNESS 1

This fellow said he was able to destroy the temple and to rebuild it in three days.

CAIAPHAS

The defendant may reply.

JESUS

The world is made of quicksilver, and things that may seem impossible today will not always be so.

CAIAPHAS

Call Witness No. 2.

> (WITNESS 2 *stands forward*)

What have you to report about the conduct of the defendant?

WITNESS 2
He said we could do anything we liked on the Sabbath.

CAIAPHAS
Has the defendant a reply?

JESUS
What did God do on the seventh day of creation? Went fishing perhaps? Played with the dust and wondered what he could make of it? Invented aspirin from a willow-tree to cure his six days headache? He was certainly not lying on his back or singing a hymn.

CAIAPHAS
I hope everyone is noting these remarks. In the meantime, call Witness No. 3.

(WITNESS 3 *comes forward*)

Please give us your testimony.

WITNESS 3
I heard him say we must give half of all our income to Caesar.

CAIAPHAS
The defendant may make a response.

JESUS
Were you well coaxed in this lie? We should give to Caesar what is due to Caesar, which may be a quarter, a tenth, a hundredth of our income, or even a negative quantity, depending on our political beliefs.

CAIAPHAS
I have myself a final question. Are you the Messiah, the Son of God?

JESUS
You must not put words into my mouth. I have said before, and in

public, that I am the Son of Man. Make of that what you will. You know that I have certain powers, otherwise I would not be here on trial. Through my words I have access to other and greater powers which will manifest themselves in time.

CAIAPHAS

I think you have said all that is needed. Are there any other witnesses? No? I shall ask Jethro to move the discussion towards a verdict.

JETHRO

My first reaction is that the defendant shows an inadmissible arrogance. I say 'inadmissible' because although it is acknowledged that he has effected some remarkable cures, both physical and mental, among the people, he is not content to be regarded as a healer, and puts on the mantle of preacher and prophet. He preaches some extreme and paradoxical doctrines which agitate and puzzle the populace. He is not even, as I understand it, a rabbi. He expresses a familiarity with God that I personally find indecent and indeed criminal. I cannot vote in his favour.

CAIAPHAS

Reuben, what do you have to say?

REUBEN

Jesus is a man of considerable magnetic force. We do not have too many speakers in Palestine who have his ability to focus complex issues into a pithy story or statement. If he was not such a revolutionary, he could be praised as an asset to our society. But I have to say, as a Scribe, that I do not believe him when he claims he is not out to destroy the law and the prophets. I think he is. It is as if he wanted a new law, a new dispensation, a new testament, and this I cannot endorse.

CAIAPHAS

Thank you, Reuben. Ezra, what is your verdict?

EZRA

As a Sadducee, I believe in the armour-plated sacredness of the temple and its rituals and sacrifices. Anyone who comes along to shoot holes in that sacredness, and even to mock it, as Jesus has done, by invading and smashing our immemorial temple business, has no place in our society.

CAIAPHAS
My own final comment would be that there is now a clear threat to priestly authority. This man speaks and acts, we are told, with authority, but where that authority comes from, he will not say. When pressed, he talks in riddles, or answers questions with questions, or simply refuses to answer. He refers to his heavenly father, who is in fact the father of us all, as we Jews believe. Even Jesus has a prayer which begins 'Our father . . .', not 'My father . . .' In all this he sails too close to the wind not to be accused of the sin of blasphemy, surely the worst of all sins. I am sure that I sum up the feeling of the court by calling for the death sentence.

JESUS (*interjects*)
– which was decided before this farce began –

(*Some policemen and priests angrily slap* JESUS *about, shouting and spitting in his face. 'Stop him!' 'Kill him!' 'Shut his mouth!'* CAIAPHAS *lifts his hand to quell the uproar.*)

CAIAPHAS
The verdict of the court has been made clear, and has been accepted. (*Cheers*) Since the law does not permit us, as Jews, to carry out the death sentence, I shall now hand the accused over to the Roman authorities, who have no such inhibition. Our strong recommendation is for this man to be executed in the manner of Roman law. (*Cheers*)

(*Exeunt, jostling and mocking the bound* JESUS *as he is led away.*)

Act Five Scene One

A room in the house of MARY, *mother of Jesus.* MARY, HELEN, MARY MAGDALENE, *and* JOHN *are talking about imminent events.*

MARY

The world is full of rumours. I asked you to come here today because you are the three who are closest to my son and will tell me the truth, if there is truth to be told. Dear John, is there news?

JOHN

There is, and there is not. But what there is, I shall tell you. As you know, he was arrested at Gethsemane, and the hierarchy of priests set up a court to try him. He is still in custody, but he managed to smuggle out a letter, which I'll read to you. (*produces small scroll, unrolls it, reads*) 'The trial is over, the first trial, there is more to come. I am giving this to a young guard who is sympathetic to me, and I hope he will find a means of delivering it. Things took their course as I had expected. Caiaphas presided.

MARY (*interrupts*)

Caiaphas! He was never a friend to my son!

JOHN (*continues reading*)

The outcome was never in doubt. He tore his robes and gave the verdict of blasphemy. He will hand me over to the Romans for final judgement. There was a lot of shouting and scuffling. I was knocked about a bit, but nothing serious. Some of them spat on me.

HELEN

In a court of law! Barbarians!

JOHN (*reading*)

The Romans will finish the process, of that I am sure. The course of events moves step by step towards my death. That is as it must be.

MARY M.

Oh no!

JOHN (*reading*)

Time is short. I have this to say. John, my beloved disciple, look after my mother, be a son to her. She will be both poor and lonely. Helen, look after our daughter, better than I ever did. It is good that something of me will be carried forward into the world. Mary Magdalene, best of friends, remember me, and be a witness to what I have done. Mother, you know that you have not yet seen the worst. Be strong. I ask it.' (*stops reading*) That is all he says in the letter.

(HELEN *and* MARY MAGDALENE *show their emotion, perhaps wiping away a tear, but there is no weeping and wailing. The women are strong, and the news is not wholly unexpected. The mother, old, stoic, stony-faced, sits motionless until speech is forced from her.*)

MARY

They took Jude from me, and now they take Jesus. How much tribute is there still to pay in this dark place, this world of dust and blood? Why are we made, if it is only to suffer?

JOHN

We have to wait, in order to know. Your son may be in chains, but I believe suffering and death are in chains too, though they do not know it.

HELEN (*practical again*)

Is there nothing we can do? Is there an appeal? Other witnesses?

MARY M.

What are the disciples doing? They are suddenly very quiet. John?

JOHN

They are in shock, dismayed, disoriented. Judas and Simon have disappeared, Judas not surprisingly, as the chief betrayer. Peter has denied he ever was a disciple. This will pass, but at the moment there is no force, no centre, no action. Could this be? Should this be? Jesus had an innate sense of what was going to happen. He warned us more than once that he would not always be with us. His nerve-ends were electric. He felt the future. We only half believed him. He is young, strong, vigorous. Why should he die? How should we have tried to protect him – with blades and bludgeons? That was not his style.

HELEN

You make it sound as if he had a death-wish. A too conscious martyr, like Antigone in the Greek play.

JOHN

From what I know of Antigone, she was only doing what she thought was right. Death was a consequence, not an aim.

HELEN

Jesus saw that play and was much struck by it. What you say is true enough. I never really took to that heroine, but yes, you are right, it was not a death-wish.

JOHN

Nor is it with him. What you know is coming, and accept, after God knows how many struggles – he went through hell in the garden of Gethsemane – that is not something you long for, believe me. You asked if there was any appeal against sentence. Whatever a lawyer might say, the brief answer is no. He has gone too far. Our only hope is that the Roman governor has still to speak, and he is an unknown quantity.

MARY M.
Pontius Pilate?

JOHN

Yes. He is a man of moods. Some people call him Mr Enigma. He has done some cruel things in the past, and no Jew is going to idealize a Roman procurator. But he's not the worst. He is certainly interested in holding onto the concordat between Rome and Jerusalem –

MARY M.
– which will hardly help the present case! –

JOHN

– No, it won't. Jesus is like a bird which has flown up from the net of that concordat, and there are fowlers on both sides who want to catch him.

MARY M.

Isolation! O my dear Jesus, disciples on the run, Jews and Romans in hideous collusion to shoot down that bird, roast it on a spit, devour it, scatter the bones to the jackals – is this to be the end of all your goodness and hope? Once I was so wretched, so beaten about by life, that when you spoke to me and drew me out of my depression, out of my tears and groans, it was as if I had been raised from the dead. If we cannot save you, we can praise you, and that to the end of time. Oh, if time remembers us – you – me – John – Helen – and my namesake your mother – or will we all roll like grains of nameless sand across eternity?

JOHN

We shall be remembered.

HELEN

How can you know?

JOHN

Trust me.

MARY

Children, you must leave me for a while. I have to rest. I have to come to terms. I have to pray. Keep me in touch with everything that is happening. God will bless us if he can.

Act Five Scene Two

A room in the home of PONTIUS PILATE, *governor of Judea.*
Rather splendid, in the Roman style. PILATE *and his wife* PROCULA
are sitting at a table. A servant is clearing breakfast away.

PILATE

Now what was that stupid dream you began telling me about? You
know I don't like interrupting breakfast.

PROCULA

My dear, it was not stupid. I know it's an old joke that 'Romans'
rhymes with 'omens', and maybe we are a superstitious people, but
this was as clear as day, and you had better listen to it. This morning you are going to a trial where you have to pass judgement on
the Nazarene preacher, is that right?

PILATE

Yes yes, I know.

PROCULA

Don't do it.

PILATE

Don't do what – go, or pass judgement?

PROCULA

Both. Either. If you feel you must go, refuse to examine this man.

PILATE

How could I possibly refuse the examination? It is my duty. You
know that perfectly well. It's on the list for today.

PROCULA

Well, if you have to examine him, find him innocent.

PILATE

Woman, I cannot find him innocent if he is guilty.

PROCULA

Of course you can. What are governors for? But in this case he actually *is* innocent, and something terrible will happen to us, and to Rome, if you condemn this man.

PILATE (*sighing*)

Oh all right, tell me why.

PROCULA

I dreamt I was walking in our courtyard, where the trees and statues are. As I was passing the bronze statue of Mercury, he raised his arm and pointed his wand at our palace, and then he spoke, in a strange metallic voice, but perfectly clear:

> The Nazarene preacher accused of heresy
> Is guilty of nothing more than hearsay.
> The Nazarene accused of insurrection
> Has no interest in that direction.
> Kill the Nazarene, kill the peace.
> Save Rome and order his release.

PILATE

My dear Procula, just because you wake up with a bit of verse in your head, you must not imagine the messenger of the gods has delivered it. Don't you think Mercury as divine messenger would be more likely to regard Jesus as a rival, and would be glad to see the back of him? Women never think these things through. If your sleep is going to be disturbed by such fantasies, I'll get the doctor to prescribe something for tonight.

PROCULA

Men are so pigheaded. You think logic rules the world? I tell you – and mark my words – this man is more important than how you see him, as a name on a list. I woke sweating from that dream, and it did not vanish in daylight.

PILATE

Sweat proves nothing, and that's the truth.

PROCULA

What is truth?

PILATE

My dear wife, we don't have time to debate metaphysics. I must get myself robed and ready; I shall go to the justice chamber; I shall question this man; I shall assess him and give my verdict; and I shall come back and tell you how guilty he was.

PROCULA

You are in the pocket of the high priest. You have had Caiaphas to dinner.

PILATE

By all the gods, what has got into you?

PROCULA

It must be the Nazarene. Go on, do your duty. Supper at seven.

Act Five Scene Three

The Roman hall of justice, with an open piazza where the public can congregate and listen. PILATE *is seated, surrounded by legal officials and soldiers. It is early morning. Enter* JESUS, *bound, guarded by two soldiers.*

PILATE (*looking closely at* JESUS)
   So you are the man? Caiaphas told me
   We had a heretic, a revolutionary, or both
   On our hands, a danger to the temple
   (With which I am not concerned) or to the state.
   If it is the latter, I express some surprise
   To see no followers, no elite band
   Of malcontents with a grenade or two.
   I don't hear 'Down with Rome!' or 'Get Pilate!'
   Yet I was told you had disciples?

JESUS
  I have. Some fled. Pressure from both sides
  Was great. They were not armed. Make no mistake:
  They will be seen again, in Palestine,
  In Syria, in Greece, in Italy,
  Armed with the Word, but not to shed blood.

PILATE
  What is this Word? What language is it?

JESUS
  Word of the world, Word of all languages.

PILATE
  I thought the Jews were local, clannish, chosen?

JESUS
  There are Jews and Jews. I am what I am.

PILATE
  And what is that? You speak with assurance.
  Are you what the court charge says you are,
  Rex, Basileus, King of the Jews?
  That is at least three languages.

JESUS
  Who put you up to this question?
  Am I to believe you thought it for yourself?
  Where is my throne, my orb, my sceptre?
  Where are my pages and my equerries?
  Have you seen me with my Maundy money
  Smiling, or knuckling a chunky topaz
  For those on their knees to lout and kiss?
  I tell you, Pilate, I have a kingdom
  But it is not of this world. If it was,
  My followers would not have been elusive,
  They would be hacking at your palace gates
  And running riot through the wretched temple.
  I almost said I sometimes wish they were,
  But only almost, so I have not said it.

PILATE

  Nevertheless you say you are a king,
  Whether of this world or another.
  One who has a kingdom is a king.

JESUS

  You say so. I have not said so.
  Truth is everything. I testify to it.
  Those who have ears to hear, they know the truth.

PILATE (*sardonically, ending the conversation*)
  What is truth?
  (*to the crowd:*) I do not see this person
  As a criminal, or as a danger to society.

VOICES

  He is! He is both! Punish him! Crucify him!

PILATE

  I have another prisoner, a bandit,
  An anarchist by the name of Barabbas.
  I shall release one of the two.
  Which shall it be?

VOICES

                    Barabbas! Not Jesus!

PILATE

  You seem very determined. But as for me,
  I have not yet given out my verdict.
  This, if he is guilty, will lead to crucifixion.
  I shall retire a moment by myself.
  In the meantime, scourge the prisoner.

  (PILATE *retires to an inner room.* SOLDIERS *seize* JESUS, *flog him
    severely, make a rough crown from a thorny branch in the
    courtyard and set it on his head, pressing it down viciously.
    They mill round him, mocking and hitting him, saying 'Hail,
    King of the Jews!'* PILATE *re-emerges, looks hard at* JESUS,
                    with curiosity rather than pity.)

PILATE
  You know I have power to stop this.

JESUS
  You have no power unless it is given to you.

PILATE
  You think a god is going to stop me?

JESUS (*is silent, but stares very hard at* PILATE)

PILATE (*To the crowd*)
  It is your last chance to set Jesus free.

VOICES
  Crucify him! Set Barabbas free!

PILATE (*to* SOLDIERS)
  Take him away. This is a matter of state.
  There will be no new kingdom in Judea.
  Crucifixions come and go. Away with him.
  Bring me a bowl of water and a napkin.
  I shall wash him right out of my life.

  (SERVANTS *bring what he asks. He washes slowly and carefully,
  looking up as he finishes.*)

Act Five Scene Four

*On the road to Golgotha. A crowd making a gradual procession up
the hill. Sense of expectation. Talking; occasional laughing; some
swearing and mocking.* JESUS *and the two* CRIMINALS *who are to be
crucified with him struggle through the crowd, each carrying the
cross-bar of his crucifix (the massive central stakes, which could*

not be carried, are already in place on the hilltop). JESUS, *now in
his own clothes, is weakened by his scourging, and stumbles badly,
at one point nearly dropping the cross-bar. A Roman* SOLDIER,
seeing this, comandeers a member of the crowd to help JESUS.
It is KOHATH, *eager to see the culmination of his activities.*

SOLDIER

You – take the bar. Take it from the man. The poor bugger is all
washed up, he can hardly walk.

KOHATH

I can't lift the bar. My muscles are not used to it. I don't do
physical work.

SOLDIER

You'll do what I tell you to do. I am in charge of this operation,
and it is going to go as smoothly as I can make it. So do what I say,
and smartly. Who do you think you are?

KOHATH

I am Kohath. I have friends in high places. I know people in the
government, people in the temple. Everyone knows me. Kohath.

SOLDIER

Mate, I don't know you from Adam. Will you take up that fucking
cross.

KOHATH (*panicking*)

I can't. I won't. You can't do this to me.

SOLDIER

Can't I?

(*The* SOLDIER *jabs his spear into* KOHATH's *stomach.*
KOHATH *screams and falls. It is a fatal blow. The* SOLDIER
*picks on someone else in the crowd, who hastens to comply.
The procession moves on.*)

Act Five Scene Five

Golgotha, the place of crucifixion. A crowd. JESUS, *a* CENTURION,
SOLDIERS, CITIZENS, PRIESTS *and* SCRIBES, *two* BANDITS, MARY *the
mother of* JESUS, MARY MAGDALENE, HELEN, JOHN. *The upright of
the cross is already in place. The cross-bar is laid on the ground,
and* JESUS, *after being stripped, is nailed to it. One of the soldiers is
inexperienced, and the* CENTURION *in charge speaks angrily to him.*

CENTURION
   Not through the palms, you fool. Through the wrists. The hand
   would simply tear with the weight of the body. Didn't they tell you
   anything at headquarters?

*(The young soldier completes the task, and the cross-bar and body
are lifted up and fixed to the upright. Huge nails through the ankles
secure the body to it.* JESUS *cries out briefly as his body takes the
strain (as* SATAN *had predicted). The two* BANDITS *are then
crucified and set in position on each side of* JESUS. *They also cry
out, and begin to taunt him. A plaque attached to the top of the
cross reads* JESUS OF NAZARETH KING OF THE JEWS.*)*

1 BANDIT
   If you're so great and powerful, why don't you get off the cross
   and get us off too?

2 BANDIT
   You're no king! Kings don't end up with nails through their wrists.
   You're a phony.

*(The crowd take up the onslaught, some laughing, sneering, and
pointing.)*

1 PRIEST
   This is the man who said he could rebuild the temple in three days.
   Fat chance!

2 PRIEST
   Can you not save yourself? Then we might believe you are a
   saviour.

(Meanwhile, at the foot of the cross, the SOLDIERS *on duty are dividing the clothes of* JESUS *among them, rolling dice for the best items.)*

1 SOLDIER
A double six for the seamless tunic!

2 SOLDIER
Marcus, you always were the jammy one.

(Standing apart is JESUS's *family group:* MARY, MARY MAGDALENE, HELEN, *and* JOHN. *They watch silently. No one breaks down, despite the horror of the scene.* JOHN *has his arms protectively around the three women.)*

(It gradually grows dark. Perhaps a storm is brewing. Something about the atmosphere, plus a climax of pain, added to a dreadful sense of alienation and humiliation, forces JESUS *to exclaim, in his own Aramaic tongue.)*

JESUS
Eloi, Eloi, lema sabachthani?

1 CITIZEN
What's he saying?

2 CITIZEN
He's calling on God. 'Why have you abandoned me?', that's the gist of it. It's Aramaic, not Hebrew.

3 CITIZEN
It's a terrible thing to say. How does he know it's not a part of God's plan?

2 CITIZEN
How would *you* feel on the cross? The fact that he's using his own native tongue shows it really comes from the depths, it has to be taken seriously.

3 CITIZEN
You were mocking him with the rest of us.

2 CITIZEN

Yes. Well. I'm not mocking him now. All right?

(*A clap of dry thunder, followed by lightning, but no rain. It is now quite dark.* JESUS *utters a loud cry – his last. The body strains, twists, and slumps. The* CENTURION, *whose job is now over, inspects the body and is assured that there is no life in it. He remarks, to no one in particular:*)

CENTURION

I have seen many deaths, but none quite like this. That clap of Jupiter's thunder seemed to come from some other universe. Very strange. (*to his soldiers:*) Right, men. That's us. Back to barracks. Break the legs of the two bandits before you go. They'll be dead by nightfall.

(*The men obey, to deep groans from the bandits. The crowd drift off, the show is over.* JESUS*'s family group are left, with the three crosses.*)

Act Five Scene Six

A quiet, secret place. Night. Enter NICODEMUS *and* JOSEPH OF ARIMATHEA.

NICODEMUS　　It is finished.

JOSEPH A.　　Finished, and begun.

NICODEMUS　　Dreadful the end.

JOSEPH A.　　Which had to be.

NICODEMUS　　Who will remove the body?

JOSEPH A.　　I will remove the body.

NICODEMUS　　You have a place?

JOSEPH A.　　I have a tomb.

NICODEMUS　　Spices.

JOSEPH A.	Linen.
NICODEMUS	Oils.
JOSEPH A.	Everything must be excellent.
NICODEMUS	Exemplary.
JOSEPH A.	Washed.
NICODEMUS	Washed, like the earth.
JOSEPH A.	Let the earth lie in the rain.
NICODEMUS	Of love, let it lie.
JOSEPH A.	Love will fall.
NICODEMUS	Like sweet rain.
JOSEPH A.	What is our duty?
NICODEMUS	To bear witness. To close.
JOSEPH A.	To close, or to open.
NICODEMUS	Wherever we may be.
JOSEPH A.	I go to the Tin Islands, To foggy Britain, to plant a tree.
NICODEMUS	I shall find an old tree To sit under, in Palestine Beneath the stars.
JOSEPH A.	Even in fogland I shall look for the stars, Nicodemus.
NICODEMUS	Look hard, look long. I shall think of you, Joseph.

Epilogue

A mountain observatory in Persia. Night. Stars. Enter GASPAR, MELCHIOR, *and* BALTHAZAR, *astronomers. Wine is circulated.*

GASPAR

We meet again. Your health, Melchior.
Your health, Balthazar. (*They clink glasses*)

MELCHIOR

And yours, Gaspar. It is a clear fine night,
Good for stars, good for us. Frosty, mind you,
But Persia relishes both hot and cold.
You've been elsewhere, you've been travelling?

GASPAR

   I've been in hot and dusty Palestine,
   Searching ancient records which in fact
   Yielded nothing. They are wedded to myth,
   These Hebrews. Not one could polish a lens.

BALTHAZAR (*laughing*)

   Are you going to damn them for that?
   Each to his own. Come to Arabia
   And we could tell you things about sand
   You cannot even imagine.

GASPAR

                          Sand?
   Do I even want to? Sand is for camels.

BALTHAZAR

   You see, Melchior? Ignorance is everywhere!
   In Egypt they used sand to raise their obelisks.

MELCHIOR

   Can we believe it? You are having us on.

BALTHAZAR

   Would a scientist play with you?

GASPAR

   Answering a question with a question
   Is unPersian, I had enough of that
   In Palestine! But let us move on.
   Some day in the future we shall have
   A round table on sand. (*All rock with laughter*)
   As I was saying, I found Palestine
   A blank for my research, but Palestine
   Has thrown down a whole brace of gauntlets
   Taunting researchers to the end of time.
   I think the three of us will still remember
   That baby in the cave in Nazareth
   Those years ago? Well, destiny is strange.

The mother has now outlived her son:
He has been ground between the millstones
Of Rome and Jerusalem, and is dead.

MELCHIOR
But how, and why?

GASPAR
                        He became a preacher,
Was thought to be a prime iconoclast,
A danger to all parties, an unknown force.
The Romans gave him their most shameful death,
Crucifixion, but the Jews – and this is weird –
Helped to press the button. The very public
Which earlier had flocked to lap up his words
Shouted for his demise, demanded it.

MELCHIOR
The old incomprehensible Middle East?

BALTHAZAR
Did the Jews not want a liberator,
A Messiah, a national leader?

GASPAR
Who knows? They certainly did not want
That Messiah. They made a great protest
To Pontius Pilate himself, the governor,
About the inscription at the head of the cross:
JESUS OF NAZARETH KING OF THE JEWS.
I thought Pilate was beautifully cool.
'What I have written, I have written,' he said,
And that was that.

MELCHIOR
                        And was that that?
No insurrection, no blood on the streets?

GASPAR
No insurrection, but a resurrection
If you believe the stories.

MELCHIOR

What!

BALTHAZAR

How?

GASPAR

They say the stone that closed his burial-place
Was rolled away, by no human hand,
And that the tomb was found to be empty
Apart from some discarded grave-wrappings.
The man himself was said then to appear
To women first, and then to his disciples,
Talking, walking, even eating, but also
Able to glide through doors like a ghost.
One of the disciples who was sceptical,
Put his finger into one of the wounds.
Does a ghost have wounds? Don't answer!
Jesus once said nothing is impossible
To the ruler of the universe (if he or she
Exists, which is extremely dubious,
I add by way of parenthesis).
Nobody dared to challenge the man
On the two by two may equal five question.
Nobody thinks things through in that country.
All is gesture, emotion, ritual.

MELCHIOR

Gaspar, you are too hard. Come to India.
Relax. No one on earth can 'think things through'.
Whole worlds can be destroyed and be reborn.

GASPAR

That is philosophy. This is life.
This man did live, did die. Even in death
He kept his reality, his iconoclasm
Provokingly bright: his all-male disciples
Fretted and fumed that he burst the grave
To talk to two women and not them.
So what do you reckon? Oh, and I forgot,

After all this he vanished, left them *that*
To think about. There is no body.
That is what they say in Palestine.

BALTHAZAR
Who told you these things?

GASPAR
                              Gradually,
From many, I gleaned it. Conversations,
Rumours, letters, not widespread yet
But growing, like a new kind of lichen
On the dead rocks of the Judean wilderness.

BALTHAZAR
In my Arabian wilderness we see
Not lichen but mirage, and then mirage
Upon mirage, a flicker like a B-film
Not to be believed.

MELCHIOR
                              In India too
There is a hideousness of falsities,
Fakirs unrolling their beds of nails,
Beggars piping to deaf snakes,
Illiterate nuns in mantra-land.
Sitting here in this great observatory
We are open to everything in the heavens
But we do not tell lies about it.

GASPAR
Of course. Of course. Nor shall we, ever.
Truth is itself a star to steer by.
But sometimes – oh, it's like a chestnut-fall,
The old rough prickly casing slips away
And a new brown shining eye peers out
Without a blink, without a history –

BALTHAZAR
That's nonsense, it always has a history!

GASPAR

    All right, but it's ready for a history
    No one can foresee, it's suddenly there.
    Now what will you do with me, it says.

MELCHIOR

    Roast it! Make a conker!

BALTHAZAR

                        Thread it
    On a necklace!

GASPAR (*laughs*)

                   My friends, you are hopeless.
    I wash my hands of you. You have no soul.
    Let me just warn you that this person,
    This Jesus, who is also called Christ,
    This dead man who may not be dead
    Already has followers called Christians.
    They are going to be blown about the world
    Like seeds – they hope –

MELCHIOR

                     O let them blow
    To India, no germination there.

BALTHAZAR

    Arabia will smother that fantasy.

GASPAR

    Well, we shall see. In the meantime I see
    A patch of stars is ready for attention
    In Persia. Gentlemen, to your posts.
    The stars and planets in their glorious courses
    Awaken thoughts that pass eternity.
    The bones of Jesus lie in Palestine.
    If they have light, let it join all our light.

First Performance

First performed by Raindog at the Tramway, Glasgow, 20 September – 7 October 2000 with the following cast:

Stevie Allen	Kohath, Menemhet
Kirsty Cox	Susanna, Woman of Samaria
Kate Dickie	Helen, Junius, Salome
Joyce Falconer	Mary Magdalene, Ruth
Andrew Flanagan	Judas Iscariot
Frank Gallagher	Satan, Jethro, Valerius
Kay Gallie	Melchior, Ezra
Paul Thomas Hickey	Jesus of Nazareth
Danny Jackson	Simon, John
Alexa Kesselaar	John the Baptizer, Joanna, Procula
Erin McCardie	Anna
Mandy Mathews	Jude
Marc Oliver	James, Captain of the Royal Guard, Matthew
David Paisley	Simon the Zealot
Iain Pearson	Nahum
Barbara Rafferty	Gaspar, Satan, Nicodemus, Caiaphas
Bob Rafferty	Jo, Andrew
Patricia Ross	Balthazar, Mary, Herodias, Joseph of Arimathea
Ronnie Simon	Agathon, Marcius, Reuben
Laurie Ventry	Joseph, King Herod Antipas, Pilate, A Roman Commandant
Jude Williams	Shaz, Peter

Additional characters played by members of the cast and supporting actors.

Director	Stuart Davids
Designer	Kenny Miller
Lighting Designer	Paul Sorley
Producers	Robbie Allen and Lee Davidson

The production was made possible with funding from the following: Tramway, the New Millennium Experience Company, Coca-Cola, the Scottish Arts Council and Glasgow City Council.